BETWEEN MAULE AND AMAZON

ARNOLD J. TOYNBEE

Between Maule and Amazon

London
OXFORD UNIVERSITY PRESS
NEW YORK   TORONTO
1967

Oxford University Press, Ely House, London W.1

GLASGOW NEW YORK TORONTO MELBOURNE WELLINGTON
CAPE TOWN SALISBURY IBADAN NAIROBI LUSAKA ADDIS ABABA
BOMBAY CALCUTTA MADRAS KARACHI LAHORE DACCA
KUALA LUMPUR HONG KONG TOKYO

Preface

THE AMAZON is the Amazon; the Maule River was once the southern frontier of the Inca Empire. The Maule's name is not familiar, as the Amazon's is, because, for the last three centuries and more, the Inca Empire and its frontiers have been ancient history. Still, the Maule River, unlike the Amazon, is historic, and I felt a thrill when my plane shot over it, en route from Santiago for Southern Chile. When I set eyes on the Maule, it gave me the same surprise as the Thames once gave to a visitor from the United States who was sitting opposite an old friend of mine in a train travelling from London to Oxford. Not far short of Oxford there is a stretch of the line on which it keeps on crossing and recrossing the Thames. 'What is that little creek?' the American asked my friend. 'The Thames.' 'Not the famous Thames?' 'Yes, the famous Thames,' and, at this, the American explorer collapsed. How could a river that was so brimful of history as the Thames was— how could this historic river fail to be at least as big as the Mississippi? My reaction to the modest dimensions of the Maule River was the same. A British tourist in Greece in the reign of the Emperor Hadrian would have been equally surprised to find that the number of cubic feet of water discharged per second by the famous Ilissos was no match for the volume of the then still unsung Thames.

'Between Maule and Amazon' is not a literally accurate description of the area covered by my travels in 1966.

Travelling southwards in Chile, I overshot the River

Maule; I almost reached the south-east corner of Chiloé Island, which was beyond the Inca empire-builders' horizon. On the other hand, all that I saw of the Amazon on this expedition was the estuary of the southernmost arm of the Amazon's huge delta, at the point where this flows below the ramparts of the Portuguese fort at Belém. I was to have overshot the Amazon as well as the Maule; I was to have visited Manaus, a city that is the capital of Brazil's province of Amazonas, and that stands on the bank of the Amazon's principal northern tributary, the Rio Negro. I lost my visit to Manaus as the penalty for being unexpectedly 'dehydrated' at Brasília. As I record this loss in retrospect, I still feel the pang. I partially console myself by remembering that I have seen the Amazonian forest at Pucallpa, on the Amazon's southern tributary, the Ucayali River, in eastern Peru. I have described this glimpse of Amazonia in a previous book called *From East to West*. The pleasure of seeing something more of the fascinating face of this planet has always to be paid for by the pain of failing to reach some cherished objective on the far side of the ever-receding horizon.

The traveller moving northwards has not, of course, come to the end of Latin America when he arrives at the Amazon basin—not even if he has reached Manaus. Latin America is a continent and a half, and the successor-states of the former Spanish Empire of the Indies extend across Middle America right up to the southern border of the United States and indeed into the United States itself; for the autonomous Commonwealth of Puerto Rico, which is United States territory, is at the same time the Spanish Empire's nineteenth successor-state. I have therefore included in this volume some impressions of visits to Venezuela (1963), Guatemala (1958), Mexico (1953), and Puerto Rico (1962).

The contents of the book thus span Latin America from one end to the other, but, of course, they do not cover anything like the whole of it. They do not include any accounts of Colombia, Ecuador, and Peru—three Latin American countries that I have visited and have already described in *From East to West*. There are no accounts of Bolivia and Paraguay either in that book or in this; for I have not succeeded in visiting either of these two important 'Indian American' countries yet.

Contents

Illustrations

Maps

Acknowledgements and Thanks

On all the journeys of which my impressions are recorded in this book, my wife and I were travelling together. In travels, two persons amount to a great deal more than twice one. The two share the experiences and exchange notes on them, and I have had this notable advantage throughout. Neither the two of us together nor either of us singly could have afforded to pay for these long journeys out of our own pockets. We owe all these travels of ours to the generosity of governments, universities, and other institutions.

We visited Mexico and Guatemala on a travel grant from the Rockefeller Foundation. In Mexico City we were guests of the Autonomous University of Mexico. In Puerto Rico we were guests of the University of Puerto Rico on the Weatherhead Foundation. Our visit to Venezuela was arranged by the British Council. In Brazil, Uruguay, and the Argentine Republic we were state guests. In Chile we were the guests of the University of Santiago. At the same time, we were received by the Chilean Government as cordially, and were given as generous facilities by them, as if we had been officially their guests as well as the University's.

In each of the countries that we visited, we had the good fortune to be constantly assisted, and this in every way, by the British Council's local Representative and his colleagues. On many sections of this long itinerary, we had the pleasure of travelling in the company of one or other of the Council's officers. Our debt to the Council's officers abroad, as well as to the Specialist Tours Department of the Council's headquarters in London, is immeasurable.

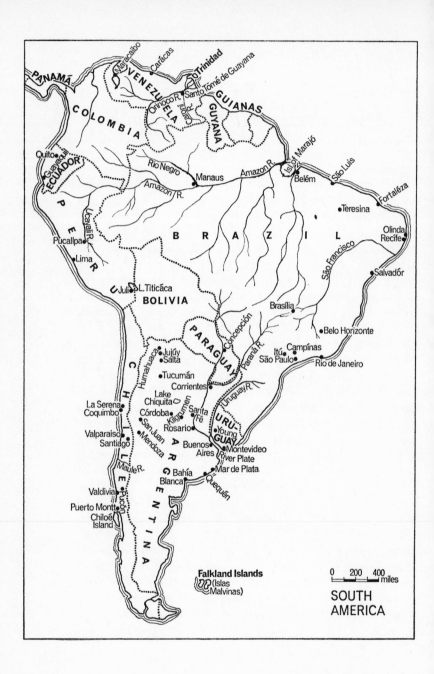

SOUTH AMERICA

Brasília versus Rio

BRASÍLIA, the reigning capital of Brazil, is only about 600 miles from the late capital, Rio de Janeiro. I say 'only' because, by Brazilian standards, any mileage in less than four figures is trivial. For distances, Brazil rivals the United States and China, and is beaten only by the Soviet Union. However, these particular 600 miles carry you from the shore of the Atlantic north-westwards into the interior of South America, and the direction makes the distance qualitatively great. I happened to arrive in Rio in a spell of cold wet weather which, I am told, was unusually harsh, even for winter-time. It seemed like the winter climate of Jacksonville, Florida; but Rio's winter norm is, I am told, more like Miami's or even Puerto Rico's. Anyway Rio, cool or warm, is always humid, whereas in Brasília the winter climate is formidably dry. In Brasília it is prudent to be imbibing something liquid all the time, even if you are not feeling thirsty. If you neglect this precaution, you may be 'dehydrated'; and, when the water is drained out of you, it carries away with it the energizing salts. Then you find your knees giving way under you. This happened to me at Brasília, and it lost me my projected visit to Manaus, the key point in the Amazon basin, where the Amazon is doubled in volume by its confluence with its giant tributary, the Rio Negro.

The violent climatic contrast between Brasília and Rio is thus of practical importance. So long as you avoid 'dehydration', the crisp clear air of Brasília, and the cool breeze that offsets the heat of the sun which bombards you out of a cloudless sky, are stimulants that will enable you to do a longer and harder day's work in Brasília than you can do in Rio with a comparable effort. But the crucial difference between the two cities is the difference in the relations between Nature and Man.

At Rio, Nature is dramatic, and she dramatizes here on the grand scale. *The* sugarloaf mountain, which appears in every picture of the city, turns out to be only one among dozens of the kind; and these huge granite cones are not Nature's only local way of being impressive. At Rio she also has, up her sleeve, a whole store of the most diverse skylines, and, where she chooses, she smothers these fantastic mountains' flanks under a dense semi-tropical forest. At Rio, Man has only two choices: either he can work in harmony with Nature or he can commit impertinences against her—and these human impertinences show up Man's limitations; for they are singularly ineffective. An album of sketches of Rio, made during the first half of the nineteenth century, shows you Man still sufficiently over-awed by Nature here to preserve his good manners. By a happy chance, Rio's oldest public monuments were built in the Baroque Age, and the Baroque is a style that chimes in with Nature's local flamboyance. How beautifully Rio's ancient churches and monasteries fitted into the unspoilt landscape. During Rio's first three centuries and a half, Nature and Man lived in harmony there. During the last hundred years, on the other hand, Man has rashly asserted himself, and this escapade of his has quickened its pace, *pari passu* with modern Man's accelerating acquisition of all kinds of new forms of technical 'know-how'. Man has now run a cable (hauling cable-cars) up to the summit of *the* sugarloaf, and he has perched a little building on the crown of the giant's head. This building looks like one of those paper caps that the passengers on a pleasure cruise put on self-consciously on the 'gala' night. But the sugarloaf mountain does not look self-conscious; he pays no more attention to what Man has done than a sleeping hippopotamus pays to the vulgarian who pokes him with an umbrella. The low but shapely headland on which the Gloria church stands has been impertinently separated from the sea by a belt of filled-in land, yet the little headland still draws the eye, as it used to do when the waves were washing its foot. The harmony between headland and church is something that cannot be spoilt. As for Rio's high buildings, they are tall only when measured by the stature of a human being; measured by the stature of the mountains between which they have been inserted, the tallest of them are still pygmies.

Thus, in Man's modern clash with Nature at Rio, Nature has won an effortless victory. By contrast, at Brasília, there has not even been a clash. Man was master here from the moment when, in the person of President Kubitschek, he chose to plant a capital city in this hitherto virgin wilderness. The chosen site is on the watershed between three river basins—those of the Amazon, the Rio de la Plata, and the San Francisco. A more important fact about this site is that it lies in the middle of the huge Brazilian plateau—a rolling country of barren red earth, whose natural covering of vegetation is a scrub that only half conceals the nakedness of the land. This undulating, scrubby, red plateau rolls on for hundreds and hundreds of miles. It is like a huge submissive animal that has waited passively for ages, always expecting Man to make his appearance one day in order to work his masterful will. The plateau has never dreamed of putting up a resistance. How Rio's spirited mountains would despise this humble-minded

B

plateau; yet the plateau, too, has a majesty of its own. I have never seen a landscape of such vast horizons; indeed, the name Belo Horizonte would have suited Brasília well enough if it had not been already appropriated, en route from the coast, by the capital of the State of Minas Gerais. The huge vault of sky that caps this vast vista is illumined, twice a day, first by a flaming sunrise and then by a glowing sunset. The red sky matches the red earth.

Why has Man picked out this particular spot as his site for a new city? What was the intention? Has it been fulfilled? This is a subject for another chapter.

What Brasília stands for

WHAT Brasília represents for me is Modern Man's triumph over Nature (a triumph that may have a catch in it). At Rio, the heights and the waters are Nature's; at Brasília they are man-made. The heights are buildings, not mountains; the waters are an artificial lake, not the sea. Man just chose to build, on this spot, a new capital city in a new style. There had been nothing human here before, nothing at all, to build on. The whole thing had to be started from zero. The competition for the plan for a city on this site was held in 1956. In 1966 the city was in existence—and by then it already had 300,000 inhabitants. Man used to attribute to God the power of creating by a sheer act of thought. Today, Man himself is behaving in this godlike way. Modern Man's technology is so resourceful and so high-powered that it can translate human plans, too, into achievements in a trice. Man cannot, it is true, yet create a universe in seven days, but in Brasília he has now proved that he can create a city in ten years. Man's earliest cities grew gradually and naturally out of an agricultural economy that may have been several thousand years old before it gave birth to anything urban. Brasília is not like that. It has been conjured out of an unhumanized wilderness by Man's fiat. This is something new in human history; we cannot yet foresee what it portends.

The creation of Brasília is an act of human self-assertion that is an event in the history of mankind as a whole, but the human hands that have built Brasília are Brazilian hands, and the human will that translated an idea into an act was the will of one Brazilian statesman, President Kubitschek. This maker of Brasília is now in exile; but it is easier to banish Kubitschek than to undo his work. Kubitschek's successors are now governing Brazil from a capital that Kubitschek called into existence. As they enter or leave the public buildings that he caused to be built, their eyes cannot fail to catch the inscriptions that record Kubitschek's work. The creation of Brasília has proved to be irreversible; and this is because Kubitschek's fiat was not arbitrary or capricious. It may be true that, without his intervention, the building of Brasília might have been delayed for many decades; it might even have miscarried altogether; yet, once done, it became clear that the creation of Brasília met an important national need of the Brazilian people—and not only a need, but an aspiration. The evidence for this is the astonishing number of the Brazilians who have flocked to Brasília to take part in the work. They made their way through the wilderness from the densely populated and poverty-stricken North-East; and, having once come, they have stayed, encamped in satellite towns that are not the satellites of Senhor Lucio Costa's plan, but are the improvisations of a human nature that is recalcitrant to any planner's regulations.

What was the Brazilian national need and aspiration that President Kubitschek divined when he set the building of Brasília in motion? The question is answered by the story of the Scottish knight who was carrying Robert Bruce's heart to be buried in Jerusalem. When the knight was passing through Spain, he stopped to help his fellow-Christians in a battle with the Moors. When the issue hung in the balance, the Scot hurled the casket, containing the precious heart, deep into the enemy's ranks, and then battled so furiously to recover it that, at the cost of his life, he routed the enemy and made the Christians masters of the field. Kubitschek's act was one of comparable bravado. Kubitschek hurled the capital of Brazil from the coast deep into the interior. His intention and expectation was that the Brazilian people would then follow up the migration of the capital and would consequently take possession, at last, of the huge hinterland. In order to draw the nation in this direction, some such dramatic act was needed; for, in Brazil, the conquest of the interior is a formidable task. The mineral treasures of Minas Gerais and the agricultural riches of São Paulo had, it is true, been exploited long since, but these two states are not very far from the coast, as Brazilian distances go. Kubitschek foresaw that, when once a new capital had been set up at Brasília, in the heart of the Brazilian plateau, the empty spaces would begin to fill up and the coastal regions would begin at last to communicate with each other overland, and not just by coastal shipping.

Brasília is something more than the cluster of impressive buildings that the eye can take in at one glance. An integral part of Brasília is the road to Belém—the port-city on the southernmost branch of the estuary of the Amazon. This road runs through previously trackless country for fourteen hundred miles—twice the length of the road to Brasília from Rio. Buses now ply between Brasília and Belém. The journey takes three days; the fares are cheap; the conditions are reasonably comfortable. At Belém, about 120 road-trucks are now arriving from Brasília every day. Brasília has, of course, also become a centre of air-communications. Already there is a plane once a week from Brasília to Manaus, the capital of Amazonas. There are flights between Brasília and Rio and São Paulo several times a day.

Indeed, Brasília is a child of the Air Age. Without aviation, it would have been difficult to survey the region and to choose the site; and it would have been difficult, again, to make a start with the building of the city. At the start, the building-materials and equipment, as well as the architects and engineers, had to be flown in. Next came the road from Belo Horizonte, the capital of Minas Gerais. The railway—a narrow-gauge one—is due to arrive next year. Its arrival should help to keep down the transportation-costs of the city's imported supplies. In the creation of Brasília, time has raced so fast that it has reversed the historical order of the introduction of the three main means of transport in the World in general.

President Kubitschek is now in exile, but Brasília—his creation—goes marching on in the spirit that the far-sighted ex-President originally breathed into it.

Brasília: The Winning Plan

THE competition for a plan for Brasília was held in 1956 and was won by a Brazilian architect, Lucio Costa. But, of course, this was not the very first step towards the creation of Brasília. The plan was required to fit a site that had been chosen already. This site was a more or less oblong slab of the plateau. On this vast plateau, there are, no doubt, other slabs of much the same size and shape; but this particular slab was singled out, not only for its central location, but also because, at the opposite end to the approach to it from Rio, it dug its nose into a network of ravines containing water-courses; and it was observed that, by building one short dam, it would be possible to convert these ravines into a V-shaped lake, eleven miles long from tip to tip, which would close the exit from the far end of the slab and would also flank the slab on either side. In the ultra-dry climate of the plateau, the creation of a large permanent body of water was a necessity of life for the great capital city that was to rise on this spot.

How was the chosen site to be used to the best advantage? This was the question that the competition was to decide. One of the reasons why Lucio Costa's plan won was, I believe, because Costa realized that, on this site, Nature was going to be unusually submissive to Man, and that therefore Man himself would have to supply here something that Nature usually imposes on him. This something was a touch of irregularity—or, perhaps one should say, subtlety—to keep Man's passion for geometry in check.

Man is a geometer. His handiwork is distinguished from Nature's work by its straight lines, perfect circles, smooth surfaces, dead-flat planes. Man's favourite angle is a right-angle. Fly over any cultivated piece of the Earth's surface and look down at the fields. Their pattern approximates to a chess-board's. Except in Iowa, the approximation is imperfect, yet the Earth's flora, when taken in hand by Man, is broken in to a much more regular pattern than you find in a virgin prairie or jungle. The comparative regularity of the pattern of the fields tells you, for sure, that they are man-made. This geometrization of Nature is one of the ways in which Man has seceded from Nature and has set up a counter-kingdom of his own. One of his works that he has geometrized, so far as Nature has allowed, is the lay-out of his cities.

'So far as Nature has allowed': this is the conditioning phrase. Many of Man's cities started as citadels. For these, Man selected natural fortresses that required a minimum of artificial strengthening; but, in revenge, Nature here imposed on Man the capricious shapes of her contours. It was not till Man could afford to lay out his cities on the plains that he could indulge his passion for geometry in town-planning. On the plain of 'Iraq and the plain of Northern China, a perfect chessboard-city could be perpetrated. (Chessboard Babylon was so depressing for Nebuchadnezzar's highland wife that he had to build her an artificial knobbly mountain—the famous 'Hanging Gardens'.) In the Mediterranean basin, Nature was more recalcitrant. When Hippodamus of Miletus laid out the Peiraeus in grid-form, Nature did him the friendly service of keeping his geometrizing propensity in check. The outline of the Peiraeus is invincibly irregular; its surface is invincibly uneven. Nature here compelled Hippodamus to break up his grid into several grids set at different angles, and, even so, there were patches that were so rocky that they defeated him. These variations that Nature imposed on the Peiraeus were the making of Hippodamus's plan, whether or not Hippodamus realized this. I fancy that he did not realize it, I fancy that he was put out by Nature's recalcitrance here; I fancy that he would have jumped at the site for Brasília, where Nature is submissive. If Hippodamus had happened to be alive in Kubitschek's and Costa's generation, I feel sure that he would have put in a plan for Brasília. But I do not believe that Hippodamus's plan would have been preferred to Costa's. Hippodamus would have offered a remorselessly symmetrical Babylon or Peking, whereas Costa's plan has introduced, by human art, the variety that, on this site, Nature for once has failed to impose.

Costa's plan has been likened to an aeroplane with bent-back wings. Costa himself prefers the simile of a drawn bow with an arrow in it. When I saw Brasília with Costa's simile in mind, the blue V-shaped lake became, in my imagination, the massive steel head of an arrow whose shaft was the main axis of Costa's city.

Senhor Costa had told me some of the points that he had had in mind when he was creating his plan. The main axis of the city must be a continuation of the road to Brasília from Rio. The traveller must find here a city that was unmistakably a capital, not just another provincial town. This capital city must not be allowed to fall apart into two cities—one official and the other residential. The public buildings and monuments and the private homes, offices, shops, and schools must be integrated into a single city. Finally, the size of city must be restricted. The population of Brasília itself must not be allowed to grow beyond about 700,000. Any surplus must be housed in satellite cities. Satellite cities have sprung up already, like mushrooms, regardless of the Costa plan. But, with this one exception, the plan is being carried out, and enough of it is already in being to enable a visitor to see the completed city of the future in his mind's eye.

The glory of creating Brasília is shared by Costa with Kubitschek.

Brasília: The Architecture

PRESIDENT KUBITSCHEK willed Brasília; Lucio Costa planned it; Costa's colleague Niemeyer built it—or, at least, built the key buildings that give Brasília its individual character.

Brasília is utterly modern. It is so modern that it has been able to do without traffic-lights, which are a distinctive feature of almost any modern city. Traffic-lights are unnecessary in Brasília because here there are no level-crossings; there are underpasses exclusively; so the flow of the traffic is never checked. The city is also modern in being dominated by its TV-mast, which soars into the sky from a mound that is the highest point in the city. This mast is the equivalent of a medieval Western city's cathedral spire—the spire which focuses the visitor's gaze at, let us say, Ulm or Salisbury. Brasília, too, has its cathedral; the part of it that is above ground is circular; it looks like some beautiful flower; but the main body of Brasília's cathedral is to be subterranean. The relation between the cathedral and the TV-mast is symbolic. Technology is the dominant element in present-day human life; religion is retreating to the catacombs again. (Question: Where is technology going to lead us, now that it has escaped from religion's control?)

At Brasília, Nature is so submissive that any style of architecture might have been imposed on the landscape. The architect could have chosen the Graeco-Roman style or the Gothic or the Baroque that has been so successful in Brazil's older cities. At Brasília the landscape would have accommodated any one of these diverse styles; it would have submitted to each and all of them meekly. However, these historic styles are associated in our minds with landscapes that are different from this one; and Niemeyer has rejected them all in favour of an ultra-modern style, with innovations that are his own creations.

The typical ultra-modern building is a vast concrete honeycomb perched on concrete stilts, and this is so abrupt a departure from all the successive styles of previous Western architecture that, when the giant honeycomb is introduced into a city that is already in being, it strikes a jarring note. At Rio, for instance, the recently built honeycombs are impertinences. They mar the exquisite harmony between the Baroque churches and the Baroque landscape there. Insert a concrete honeycomb into Venice, and you would be committing an aesthetic outrage. A completely new style demands a completely new site, where the new style will not be exposed to any odious comparisons. The site of Brasília was a *tabula rasa*, so here Niemeyer has had a free hand to see what he can make of an all-modern-style city within the framework of Lucio Costa's subtle plan.

Niemeyer's residential buildings strike an amateur's eye as being still within the ultra-modern convention. Most of the population of Brasília is housed in flats; and, in these, the honeycomb effect is enhanced by giant screens of open concrete fretwork that cover the backs of these apartment houses. (Perhaps the screens conceal the washing that is hanging out to dry.) Niemeyer's originality shows itself in the public buildings—ranging from the local primary school in one of the residential *quadras* to the congressional buildings and the government offices along the city's main axis.

To my mind, Niemeyer's gem is the presidential 'Palace of the Dawn'. This lies below the slab of plateau on which the city stands. The Palace lies near the inner edge of the lake; and the road leading to it runs at an acute angle to the city's main axis. By the time you have reached 'the Palace of the Dawn', you feel that you have left the city far behind. Yet, as you step into the Palace's entrance hall, you are surprised to see the city's skyline confronting you. This makes you turn your head to see whether you have really lost your bearings. Of course, you have not. The city's skyline is truly behind you, as you had supposed. What you are seeing in front of you is a reflection of this in a huge mirror. This contrivance symbolizes a human problem that besets the head of a state. Being human, he must escape, from time to time, from the pressure of public affairs; but, being a servant of the state, as well as a human being, he must never be allowed to forget his public responsibilities.

'The Palace of the Dawn' is a new departure in architecture, so it is not easy to give an impression of it. Its openness to the air and the light reminded me of the architecture of the Apadana—the great audience hall at Persepolis, which was once the capital of the Persian Empire. The Apadana is borne aloft by tall slender columns. The effect of this Iranian architecture, too, was something new in its day, but the shape of the columns that made this effect was not new. By contrast, Niemeyer's columns in 'the Palace of the Dawn' and in his public buildings in the city have made a break with all the traditional columns of the past five thousand years. Niemeyer's columns are not just concrete variations on tree-trunks or bundles of reeds; they are shaped like the flying buttresses of a medieval church in Western Europe. As one gazes at them, one feels that one is in the presence of a great act of architectural creation. Performed in Florence or at Chartres, this creative act might have been self-defeating. At Brasília, on the other hand, there is no ancient architecture in a different style to put Niemeyer's flying columns out of countenence. The virgin site has given its blessing to the architect's creative idea.

Belém

WHEN one flies to Belém from Brasília, the plane does not make a bee-line for its destination. It is going to call at São Luis en route; and, on the way to São Luis, it passes over Teresina, the capital of Piaui state. (At Teresina there is an airport, where a plane could make an emergency landing.) This route carries the traveller over 'the Dry Polygonal' which occupies so much of the interior of North-Eastern Brazil. As you leave Brasília, heading north-north-east, you see some signs of life below you for the first thirty or forty minutes. There are footpaths, cattle-tracks, a dirt road, even an occasional cottage. But, after that, life ceases—not only human life, but vegetation too. For hours, one passes over a landscape that is as naked as the Moon's. It is the more surprising to find oneself suddenly flying over a town on the bank of a river, and then over a larger town, straddling the same river lower down. The river is the Parnaiba, the two towns are Floriano and Teresina; and Teresina has more than one hundred thousand inhabitants. It is the capital of the state of Piaui. This big town is marooned in a landscape that is as bare as a bone.

A still greater surprise follows quickly. As the plane descends towards São Luis, you find that, abruptly, you have left the Moon-like landscape behind and are descending into a lush tropical jungle, where the rank vegetation is interrupted only by winding water-courses; and so it continues when you turn west and fly, behind the Atlantic coast, from São Luis to Belém.

Belém is an old city, and it has defeated the jungle in its immediate neighbourhood. It has defeated it so thoroughly that it has taken the trouble to preserve two relics of the vanished jungle as museum pieces. One of these is the Bosque—a patch of virgin jungle that is now a public park inside the city. The other remnant of the jungle is the cluster of huge writhing tree-roots that are tearing apart the ruins of a Jesuit church in the grounds of the Federal Agronomic Institute. This assault of the aggressive tropical vegetation on the puny works of Man is a spectacle that one can see on the grand scale at Angkor in Cambodia.

Belém is the ocean port for the navigation of the Amazon and its tributaries. It stands, about 90 miles from the open ocean, on the shore of the Bay of Marajó. The southernmost of the mouths of the Amazon debouches through this estuary. (This mouth is separated from the others by the Island of Marajó, which is said to be about the size of Belgium.)

The port of the Amazon basin! That sounds like a free pass for making a fortune; and Belém did make its fortune for a brief spell when the only rubber available for meeting a rising world-wide demand was the wild rubber that grows round the headwaters of the Amazon and its affluents. This source of Belém's wealth was two thousand miles and more away from Belém itself; and the mushroom city of Manaus quickly inserted itself, in between, near the Amazon's confluence with the Rio Negro. Yet the profits from wild rubber were so great, while the short boom lasted, that there was enough wealth and to spare for Manaus and for Belém as well. The two cities advertised their prosperity by building opera-houses of Italian marble. Since Manaus was nearer to the rubber, its opera-house is bigger and more opulent than Belém's; but Belém's, too, is opulent enough to be astonishing.

These two opera-houses, like the Bosque at Belém, are evidences of a vanished grandeur. When rubber began to be cultivated in Malaya, the Amazonian wild-rubber business collapsed; and, when once the wild rubber had lost its value, the Amazon basin, huge though it is, was not a profitable enough hinterland for Belém to buoy up the port-city's prosperity. At the moment, Belém is a city with a past. Yet who knows whether Belém may not have a future too? For the Amazon basin is so huge that, any day, it may be found to contain other natural resources, hitherto unknown and untapped. There is talk, today, of gold having been struck, far away in the interior. There might be other rare minerals too. Modern technology has a way of converting hitherto useless stuff into commercially valuable commodities.

The debris of the short-lived rubber boom is not the only economic shipwreck that one sees at Belém today. A sad sight here, for a British visitor, is the shipwreck of the local British commercial interests. There was a time when every public utility in Belém was British-made and British-owned, and when Britain was the source of all consumer-goods that were imported to meet the city's needs. Today, Belém's consumer-goods are mainly produced, inside Brazil, at São Paulo; but the section of the market that is still left for foreign enterprise is no longer held by Britain. She has been supplanted by the United States and Germany and Japan. The United States had the advantage of coming late into both world-wars and of continuing to do business, almost as usual, even after she had become a tardy belligerent. But why should Britain have allowed Germany and Japan to take her place? Germany in both wars, and Japan in the second war, were as deeply involved as Britain herself was. So why have these two countries more than recovered their previous business at Belém, while Britain has not recovered hers?

The fault lies in ourselves; and it would be a salutary lesson for slovenly British business managements and restrictive-minded British industrial workers to visit this lost market that was once theirs. Belém is not just one lost British market; it is a symbol of hundreds of others scattered all over the face of the globe. Britain's nineteenth-century prosperity was based on British markets in a thousand Beléms. As I stood on the parapet of Belém's fortress, and watched the waters of the Amazon sliding past between me and Marajó Island, I was thinking sadly of the British people's present wilful refusal to recognize that they are heading for an economic catastrophe. It is, I fear, the same attitude of mind as their wilful refusal to take the Second World War seriously till disaster descended on them in June 1940. In the Second World War, Britain was saved from destruction by the enemy's egregious mistakes, but, in the present British economic crisis, the British people's enemy is itself, and this enemy's mistakes are not going to bring Britain an unmerited salvation. Come, while there is still time, to look at the wreckage of British business at Belém. This is a less expensive stimulant for action than it would be to hire the German Army to reoccupy the Channel Ports.

c

Fortaléza and Recífe

I HAD been aware of the differences between the principal regions of Brazil: the temperate South, the dry plateau, the Amazonian tropical forest, the North-East; but I had not been prepared for the local differences within each region. I had, in fact, failed to imagine to myself the sheer size of Brazil. This is so huge that even one of Brazil's smaller regions may be as big as half a dozen European countries combined. My miscalculation misled me about the North-East. I had assumed that the North-East was homogeneous, and that, if I had seen any one of its three principal cities— Fortaléza, Recífe, Salvadór—I should have seen all three for practical purposes. Having now seen Fortaléza and Recífe and been astonished at the difference in climate, scenery, and architecture north-west and south-east of 'the Hump', I am glad that Salvadór, too, is on my itinerary.

I knew that, as compared with Belém, the North-East is comparatively dry; so, en route from Belém to Fortaléza, I was not surprised to see the tropical forest fade out not far to the east of São Luis. The hinterland of Fortaléza is decidedly dry, except for the little mountains that rise up from the plain here and there. These mountains are thickly clothed in tropical vegetation, and their flanks are washed by tumbling streams; but, in this section of the North-East, such generous moisture and verdure are exceptional. When you travel on south-eastwards from Fortaléza to Recífe, the dry country continues to the point at which one is told to fasten one's seat belt, and then one descends into a strip that is as green as the country round Belém. This coastal section of Pernambúco is not the tropical forest that I have seen in Eastern Peru and in Northern Guatemala, where the tall trees stand in such a dense array that there is not room for a dead tree to fall prostrate. All the same, the coastal section of Pernambúco is a lush green country, and the luxuriance of the vegetation here is accounted for by the drenching rain through which we viewed it. How different from the howling wind that, at Fortaléza, blows, night and day, out of a clear sky.

Thus there is a striking contrast in the physical setting of two cities that look so close to each other on the map of the World. Yet the contrast in the 'personalities' of Fortaléza and Recífe is even more remarkable. Fortaléza is a relatively modern city. The fortress from which it takes its name was built by the Dutch during their temporary occupation of North-Eastern Brazil in the seventeenth century, and the present city has grown up round the ex-Dutch fort since the Portuguese reoccupation. The population of Fortaléza has passed the half-million mark and is still increasing, though, for the casual visitor, this is an economic puzzle. How can so big a city make its living from so lean a hinterland? It is true that the majority of the population is sadly poor. One catches a glimpse of this poverty when one visits the shore and views the hard life of the fishermen who ply their dangerous trade in craft made of balsa-wood imported from the Amazonian forest. Yet a human being, however poor, must eat, and he must find some shack to shelter himself and his family. So how does the population of Fortaléza continue to grow without starving to death? Fortaléza's growth is a mystery.

The present economic condition of Recífe is even more mysterious. The city bears conspicuous marks of economic decay. Parts of its splendid harbour are being allowed to silt up. A swing-bridge over another part is out of action. The streets have been worn into pot-holes that are not being mended. This decay of the port is comprehensible; for Recífe used to import its consumer-goods from Europe and to pay for them by exports of sugar. Today the consumer-goods come to Recífe from São Paulo overland, and the sugar industry, I am told, has failed to keep up with the times. Recífe's past commercial prosperity is attested by the extensive residential quarter—street after street of fine houses. But is the prosperity altogether past? Those fine houses—some of them miniature palaces—look as if they were still being well kept up; and neglected ancient buildings quickly decay in Recífe's humid climate. As one drives through this quarter, one also sees living evidence of continuing middle-class prosperity. Hundreds of schoolgirls in neat uniforms are waiting at the bus-stops; some of them are even being taken home in private cars. The port is decaying; the upkeep of the city's public services seems to be neglected by the municipal authorities; yet there are these unmistakable signs of unextinguished middle-class prosperity; and this contrasts painfully with the unhappy condition of the poor majority of the population.

The failure of the public authorities to alleviate the distress of the poor has been criticized severely by the Archbishop of Recífe, who has recently been transferred to this see from Rio. On the Government's side, and among the vocal minority of the population of Recífe itself, the Archbishop's protest has raised a storm, and a gust of this came my way. At a press conference at Recífe, I was taken aback by being asked whether Pope John XXIII had not opened the floodgates for Communism. My interrogator was, I think, tracing the local Archbishop's call for social justice back to its Roman source. The Archbishop of Recífe is assuredly a prelate of Pope John's school. My answer to the surprising question was that the new line that is being taken by the

Catholic Church, so far from being Communist, is the
alternative to Communism—perhaps the only alternative
in a Catholic country. Communism would be the penalty
for failing to repent and reform. So Pope John and his kind
are the best bulwarks against Communism, to my mind.

The critics of the Archbishop of Recífe complain that,
till recently, the Catholic Church had no more social
conscience than its critics themselves have. This is a feeble
argument. Better late than never; and, if the Church's
attitude has changed, this surely redounds to the credit of
the generation of Catholic leaders who have broken with
tradition. I do not know what the truth is about the Church's
past social record in North-Eastern Brazil. But the number and
the beauty of the churches in Recífe are evidence that, in the
past, the Church did not distribute all its funds to the poor.

One could spend many days visiting the Baroque and
pre-Baroque churches in Recífe itself. Here they are
enveloped by buildings that are relics of Recífe's nineteenth-
century prosperity. If you want to see the sixteenth-century
and the seventeenth-century ecclesiastical architecture of
North-Eastern Brazil as it was before the modern commercial age, visit Olinda, the original capital and archi-
episcopal see of Pernambúco. Olinda (about five miles distant
from Recífe) is a city set upon a hill and crowned with
churches and monasteries in the Portuguese, Spanish, and
Italian way. Here, but for the palm trees, you might imagine
yourself to be somewhere on the north side of the Mediterranean. The seventeenth-century Dutch conquerors of North-
Eastern Brazil moved the capital of Pernambúco from the hill
of Olinda down to the harbour of Recífe, and they fitted Recífe
out with canals Dutch-fashion. The Dutch were evicted, but
Olinda did not win back its lost status from Recífe, the
rival city whose fortune the Dutch had made. Olinda is
decaying, but, even in decay, it is very beautiful still.

Salvadór

I HAD been told that, among the cities of North-Eastern Brazil, I should find Salvadór to be the most beautiful, the most interesting, and the most congenial, and so I did. I daresay there is as much poverty at Salvadór as there is at Recífe. There may be more, for there was less shipping in the port, though this port lies within the huge bay that gives its name—Bahía—to the state of which Salvadór is the capital. Salvadór may be poor, but it is smiling. One does not feel, here, the social tension that pervades the atmosphere of Recífe. Perhaps this sunny way of taking poverty is a gift to Salvadór from the African element in the population. This element is strong—and strong not merely in terms of numbers. The descendants of the slaves who were imported to Salvadór from Africa have retained much more of their original African culture than their compatriots who were carried to North America. African religion is still being practised under a transparent Christian veneer, and its liturgy is still being recited in the Yoruba language of Nigeria. What is more, this African religious influence has permeated the European stratum of the population. Salvadorians of European, or partly European, descent have come to combine African nature-worship with Catholic Christianity in a symbiosis that was first worked out by their African fellow-townsmen. Recently, the University of Salvadór has established an institute for studying the local African culture and tracing it back to its origins in West Africa. If this study were to develop and were to make a popular appeal on both sides of 'the Straits of Dakar', Salvadór might become an important cultural link between the Western World and Negro Africa. This would help to bring together these two great sections of mankind; and that is a service that could not be performed by the African element in the United States; for here, in contrast to what happened in Bahía, the African slave-immigrants lost not only their personal freedom but their cultural heritage as well.

In the market at Salvadór one feels oneself to be on African ground. It reminded me of the busy market at Onitsha on the bank of the River Niger in the Ibo country in South-Eastern Nigeria. The goods—including cult objects—that are on sale have an African flavour. The difference—and it is a significant one—is that, at Onitsha, everyone is pure African in race, whereas at Salvadór the buyers and sellers include people of all shades of colour, from Black to White. At Onitsha a white skin is an object of curiosity; in the market at Salvadór, differences of colour pass unnoticed; they are effaced by a community of culture which unites Salvadorians of all colours.

In the market one finds oneself in contemporary Africa, but the market is in the lower city, close to the shore, and in the upper city, which towers above it, one finds oneself in seventeenth-century Europe. At Salvadór the hill-town and the harbour-town, which at Recífe are five miles distant from each other, are in immediate juxtaposition, and they communicate by steep zig-zagging cobbled streets. (There is also a public lift for foot-passengers.) Salvadór was the capital of Brazil in the Baroque Age, and the upper city retains the air of a capital still. Its grandeur is past, but the effect is mellowness, not melancholy. Whole streets of the former nobility's town houses are still standing intact, and in their decay they have not lost their graciousness. As for the Baroque churches, they are as numerous as in any ancient

Spanish or Italian city. The upper city of Salvadór is built, like Rome, on a cluster of hills, and each hill is crowned by a church or a monastery. The queen of them all is the church of San Francisco, and, if you happen to have a prejudice against the Baroque style, you should visit this monument to St. Francis of Assisi in Salvadór. Here the Baroque decoration is carried to a tropical extreme of luxuriance that is alien to both a thirteenth-century and a twentieth-century Western eye. Yet in this church the elaboration does not offend; for, after all, Salvadór is in the tropics, and the style is in harmony with the natural environment. As you gaze at the intricate gilded ornamentation, you will find your prejudice evaporating. When the noble seventeenth-century statue of St. Francis catches and focuses your attention, you will find yourself entering into the spirit in which this statue was carved and in which this church was designed.

The statisticians tell us that, by the end of this century, the population of the World will have grown to two or three times its present size. It may stabilize, they guess, at ten times its present size a century hence. By that time, Salvadór may have been engulfed in a continuous megalopolis that will have spread its tentacles along the coast of Brazil from Rio to Fortaléza inclusive. For the most part, this world-city of the not so remote future seems likely to be monotonously uniform. Already today, the Hilton hotels in the still separate cities of the World are as like each other as two peas. Here and there, though, some former separate city will have had a strong enough individuality to enable it still to stand out as something different from the drab mass of standardized streets and buildings around it; and one may guess that, a century hence, Salvadór will be one of these rare cultural oases in a world-wide architectural desert. This prophecy is high praise, but not higher praise than Salvadór deserves.

São Paulo

I DID not set eyes on São Paulo till September 1966, but, nine years back, I had already had an experience of this giant city's power. I had encountered São Paulo unexpectedly in the Syrian city of Homs. Here I had been in the other hemisphere and on the opposite side of the globe. Yet I had learnt that an appreciable part of the population of Homs was now in São Paulo, and I had been told that these Homsi Paulistas were prospering in the distant hive of industry to which they had found their way. My next encounter with São Paulo had been within closer range—though North-Eastern Brazil would count as being still far away from São Paulo on any European scale of distances. At Belém, on the southernmost arm of the Amazon delta, I had heard that about 120 trucks were arriving every day by the new road from Brasília—and the contents of these trucks must have come from São Paulo; for Brasília itself is a consumer, not a producer, of manufactures. Then at Recífe, on Brazil's north-eastern hump, the power of São Paulo had been impressed on me, once again, by the stagnation of this once busy port. Not so long ago, Recífe had bought its consumer-goods in Europe and had imported them by sea. Now it was buying them in São Paulo and was importing them overland. An emancipation of Brazil from economic servitude to foreigners? This is, no doubt, the account of the economic revolution in North-Eastern Brazil that would be given by a Paulista, but a Pernambucan might not see the change in this light. He might see it as being, for him, merely a change of masters. São Paulo, he might say, had snatched out of European hands the profits of exploiting him. This is how the South Italians regard the economic power of Milan, and São Paulo is the Milan of Brazil. The economic contrast, and the consequent psychological tension, between Southern Italy and Milan is familiar to European observers. Transfer Italy to the Southern Hemisphere and magnify her size many times over, and you have the present-day relation between Northern Brazil and São Paulo.

Like Milan, São Paulo is an old city—old, that is to say, on the time-scale of European settlement in the Americas. São Paulo was founded in 1554. (Milan has existed since at least the sixth century B.C.) What is peculiar to São Paulo is the amazing speed of its present industrial growth. Till far on in the nineteenth century, São Paulo was of little account by comparison with the coastal cities of Brazil, while, among the inland cities, it was overshadowed by Belo Horizonte in Minas Gerais—the adjoining inland state in which there had been a mining boom in the seventeenth and eighteenth centuries. Round about the turn of the nineteenth and twentieth centuries, São Paulo was suddenly benefited by the coffee boom in its hinterland. It made its mark first as a coffee emporium, as Belém and Manaus made their mark contemporaneously as the centres for the collection and export of the wild rubber from the headwaters of the Amazon. The coffee boom did not last much longer than the rubber boom lasted, and, with its collapse, São Paulo might have been expected to languish, as Manaus and Belém have done. Today, Belém and Manaus are living on wistful memories of their brief experience of affluence. The characteristic monuments of this there, as in the extinct gold-mining towns of Australia and the Rockies, are

the sumptuous opera-houses in which Europe's prima
donnas once deigned to sing in return for extravagant fees.
The monuments of São Paulo, however, are no such curiosi-
ties of nineteenth-century history. They are tall buildings in
the post-Second-World-War style for which the Brazilians
have a passion. São Paulo's high buildings spring from a
ridge that is the watershed between the Atlantic and the
basin of the River Paraná. When that skyline bursts into
view, one does not feel that one is looking at inanimate
erections of steel and concrete. Those gigantic creatures
seem alive; one can almost fancy that they are growing and
multiplying before one's eyes. It is as if some magic ferti-
lizer had produced a sudden out-size crop.

São Paulo claims to be the biggest city in all South
America now. Buenos Aires contests this claim, of course.
The dispute between the two cities is bound to be inconclusive, because the competing figures depend on where one
draws the line round 'Greater Buenos Aires' and 'Greater
São Paulo', and these lines are elastic. The contrast between
the two cities in style is clearer and is also more interesting.
Buenos Aires is a great modern city that has attained its
present stature gradually and naturally in the course of a
century or more. São Paulo is one of the world's wonders
that looks as if it had been conjured up instantaneously, out
of nothing, by an Arabian jinn. Both cities are attracting
additional population from far afield—not only from remote
corners of their own respective countries, but from other
parts of South America and from other continents. In the
influx into São Paulo, Pernambucans are being reinforced by
Germans, Poles, Czechoslovaks, and Japanese.

The administration of this fantastically expanding city
is a problem for its mayor. The apportionment of the tax-
yield between the Brazilian Federal Government, the government of the state, and the municipality is fixed by a federal

law, and, in this apportionment, the municipality receives short measure. With these inadequate financial resources, how is São Paulo city to keep on extending the network of its public utility services? How is it to build the underground railway that Buenos Aires possesses and that São Paulo needs? The one thing certain is that, for as far as one can see ahead into the future, São Paulo is going to continue to grow at its present break-neck speed. Financial stringency is not going to check this growth, but it seems likely to make it untidy. This may give Buenos Aires a comforting sense of superiority, yet she cannot afford to smile; for São Paulo's economic hinterland is even greater than Buenos Aires' is. When, perhaps a century hence, the two cities coalesce with each other as two nodes in a world-encompassing Ecumeno-polis, we may guess that São Paulo will stand at least a head higher than Buenos Aires above the 'conurbation' that will link them together via the basin of the mighty Paraná.

Itú

I HAD seen the lean hinterland of Fortaléza and the lush but unkempt hinterland of Recífe, and I had been left wondering how these two big cities managed to live. Recífe's sugar-plantations did not seem to be an adequate source of livelihood, and Fortaléza did not seem to have any appreciable agricultural resources of any kind. On the other hand, there was no mystery about the agricultural hinterland of São Paulo. After São Paulo had lived a life of modest obscurity for more than three hundred years, the city had suddenly had its fortune made for it by the coffee boom at the turn of the nineteenth and twentieth centuries. A glance at the map of Brazil reveals a striking difference between São Paulo state and Brazil's north-eastern hump. In the interior of the hump the place-names are spread thin, for this is 'the Dry Polygonal'; it fills the interior of the hump and confines cultivation to a few patches of fertile territory on the coast. By contrast, in São Paulo state the place-names are sown thick on the map all the way from São Paulo city to the state's north-western border along the left bank of the Paraná River. This is the land of cattle and coffee to which São Paulo owed its first bout of prosperity before its present amazing bout of expansion as an industrial city.

It had been arranged that I should have a sight of São Paulo's rich and populous hinterland. We were to arrive in São Paulo from Salvadór early on a Saturday afternoon, and to travel by car about 200 kilometres north-westward, into the interior, to spend the week-end on a fazenda (a rural estate). Till the last lap, our journey went according to schedule. We landed at Rio airport on time, and, after a twenty-minutes' halt there, we were to make the eighty-five minutes' flight from Rio to São Paulo. The plane had done well so far; it was a Caravelle; and we feared no evil. Something, however, had gone wrong with our Caravelle on landing; but, for the next four hours, the airline kept us in ignorance of the horrid truth that the plane was grounded for an indefinite time to come. When the passengers' anger finally boiled over, and the line reluctantly transferred us to one of the rival company's flights, São Paulo airport was closed by bad weather. Would it open again by the time we reached it? The weather was unkind to us, and, after circling over São Paulo in vain, our plane headed for the international airport at Campínas, one hundred kilometres away. Campínas lies north-west of São Paulo, on the road to the fazenda that was to have been our destination, and, if our would-be host could have known that we had been deposited there, he might have picked us up and carried us on. It was, of course, impossible for us to make contact with him; so, instead of travelling on north-westwards, we had to travel south-eastwards to São Paulo city by bus—and this in the dark, so that we could not see even that piece of the countryside. This was our biggest frustration since we had lost our visit to Manaus in the Amazon basin.

Should we have to leave São Paulo without getting even a glimpse of the countryside that had played so important a part in the life of the city, and consequently also in the life of Brazil? Fortunately, the last day of our stay in São Paulo happened to fall on the date of the national holiday. For lectures, round-table discussions, and other academic exercises, this was a *dies non*. We were free to go out into the country for the inside of this one day. How could we spend this limited time to the best advantage? The kind friend who was to have been our host advised us to make a circular tour via a little country town called Itú. We followed his advice, and we were rewarded.

The ridge on which São Paulo rears up its tall buildings is the watershed between the Atlantic seaboard and the basin of the Paraná River; so, when you travel inland from the city, you are at the headwaters of the numerous tributaries of the Paraná that flow north-westwards across São Paulo state. In this first zone of São Paulo's hinterland the country is a tangle of hills that are still partly covered with their original forest fleece. 'Fleece' is the right word, for this forest is the luxuriant matted forest of the tropics. São Paulo city itself actually bestrides the Tropic of Capricorn, and Itú is inside the tropical zone. Yet it had been difficult to realize that we were in the tropics on our bus-drive from Campínas airport to São Paulo. This southern fringe of the tropics had given us an English welcome on the night on which we had arrived. The air had been as damp and raw and chilly as if we had been landing on a winter day at London airport.

This hill-country round the sources of São Paulo state's western waters was not the promised land of which I was in quest. Here and there the hillsides had been cleared of forest and been planted with coffee, and an occasional open piece of ground had been planted with vines, but these patches of cultivation were rare. No doubt they would have become more numerous if time had allowed us to travel on farther down the river-valleys according to our original plan that had gone awry. Perhaps what we lost in our glimpse of agriculture was repaid to us in our taste of beauty. The upper valleys of the rivers have a natural beauty, and here, as in Europe, this has been improved upon by the works of

Man. In the immediate hinterland of São Paulo city, settlers from Europe have been cultivating the soil for four hundred years by now, and, as in Europe, in contrast to the United States, Man in this long-settled part of Brazil has treated Nature, not as an enemy to be bludgeoned into obedience to Man's will, but as a friend to be coaxed into co-operating with Man to serve Man's purposes. The result, as in Europe again, is harmony, not discord, and this harmony is expressed in the graciousness of the little country towns. These nestle in the hollows of the hills, and even the smallest is likely to have at least one beautiful building—the church perhaps, or the town hall—that dates from the seventeenth or eighteenth century. Itú is a little country town of this gracious kind. We enjoyed its beauty, and, by taking our lunch there, we also were made aware of the contrast between the prosperous South of Brazil and the poverty-stricken North-East.

Itú is a small country town with one or two modest factories on its outskirts. One of these is a brewery that was established by a German immigrant three generations ago. This brewery has gone into the restaurant business; the restaurant's fare is plentiful and excellent; the capacity is surprisingly large for so small a town; yet, on the day on which we took our lunch there, this restaurant was crammed with family parties, and a table was no sooner vacated than it was re-filled and then re-filled again by fresh relays of guests. The prices were on the middle-class scale, and all the guests looked like middle-class people. Of course, this was a festive day. But, even on the national holiday, could little Itú muster that number of professional people, shopkeepers, and factory managers? Was the German restaurant's excellence perhaps famous enough to bring visitors from Júndiai, the manufacturing town half way between São Paulo and Campínas? Did some of the lunching parties come from as

photo by Nick de Morgoli, Camera Press, London

I Brazil: Rio, the Gloria church

photo by Mike Andrews, Camera Press London

II Brazil: Brasília

far away as São Paulo itself? We could not tell. Yet, even if this excellent restaurant at Itú drew its holiday clientèle from a considerable distance, the scene that we were witnessing there would have been unthinkable in North-Eastern Brazil. The clientèle of the restaurant at Itú enjoyed a French standard of living, at least as far as eating was concerned. Our lunch at Itú was a compensation for the cotton-plantations, farther to the north-west, which we had not managed to reach, owing to our chapter of accidents on the day of our arrival. The restaurant had demonstrated to us in a practical way that, in Brazil, there are two nations with two quite different standards of living. It will be as hard for Southern Brazil to raise the North to its own level as it will be for Northern Italy to rehabilitate the Mezzo-giorno.

D

The Campo

URUGUAY is a small country, even in terms of the European scale of sizes. By comparison with its two huge neighbours, Brazil and Argentina, Uruguay is minute. In the relation between town and country, Uruguay is a miniature Australia.

In Uruguay, as in Australia, the wealth is produced in the countryside, but the people prefer to live in the city. All but a fraction of the population of Australia now lives in five cities; about half the population of Uruguay lives in Montevideo. A country of Uruguay's modest size could not maintain more than one big city, in spite of the fact that Uruguay has been endowed by nature more generously than Australia has been. Vast tracts of the Australian continent are barren. By contrast, nearly the whole of rural Uruguay consists of gently undulating grasslands, broken only here and there by outcrops of granite, with some limestone in the hills behind Punta del Este. The city of Montevideo is a parasite on this grassy campo. If the grass did not provide pasturage for cattle, the urban population of Montevideo could not survive. In other words, the campo, not Montevideo, is the real Uruguay. I was therefore eager to break my way out of the city into the countryside, and my wish was fulfilled, thanks to the kind offices of the Uruguayan Ministry of Agriculture and the British Embassy and the British Council. Out of my week in Uruguay, I was able to spend three days in the campo. I visited the Uruguayan

Government's experimental station for agronomy at Estanzuela, close to Colonia, where the ferry crosses the Rio de la Plata to Buenos Aires; I visited an estancia in the hilly hinterland of Punta del Este which specializes in breeding super-sheep; and, thanks to the Ministry of Agriculture's kindness in wafting me across country in a Cessna plane, I was able to be present at a cattle-sale on an estancia near a north-western country town called Young. (The name is Scottish, but it is pronounced like Jung, the famous Swiss psychologist.)

The livestock industry in Uruguay has now reached a crisis at the end of its prosperous first century and a half. In Uruguay, Nature has been so bountiful that, till lately, Man has been content just to live on Nature's bounty without seeking to augment it. He has taken the native grass as he found it, and has not attempted to improve the breeds of sheep and cattle that he has imported from Europe to turn the campo's natural grass coverage into meat and hides and wool. In consequence, the campo's production has remained stationary ever since the campo has been exploited up to its full natural capacity, as it has been for some time past. Uruguay cannot afford to acquiesce in a stationary economy; but, if production is to be increased beyond the present natural level, Man must become Nature's active partner. Man must take positive action for improving the quality of both the pasture and the livestock.

That is the raison d'être of the Government's experimental station at Estanzuela. This is an impressive enterprise. The staff of agronomic scientists at Estanzuela is two-thirds Uruguayan and one-third foreign, and this foreign third is recruited from a number of different nations whose agronomic experience is relevant to the local conditions in Uruguay. The three members of the staff who showed me round were an Uruguayan, a Scot, and a Frenchman. The task of improving the pasturage is approached in two different ways. One way is to enrich the native pasturage with fertilizers, and the effect of this is to enable the more nutritious plants to crowd out those that are less valuable. 'Native' is, in this context, an ambiguous word. For instance, one 'native' plant that the application of fertilizers stimulates is a clover; but this clover is native only in the sense that it is not artificially sown; it is the offspring of an original sown clover-crop that has since run wild. With the aid of fertilizers, this wild clover can drive its competitors off the field without further human aid. The alternative method is, of course, to eliminate the native pasturage and to sow foreign grasses in place of it; but this is no doubt more expensive than it is to give the native pasturage the means of improving itself.

I was gazing at a row of parallel strips, each bearing a different kind of herbage, when, in a paddock beyond, I noticed a flock of sheep, each equipped with a bag that hung down grotesquely below the animal's hindquarters. What, I asked, was the purpose of this quaint equipment? The answer was that the bag collected the sheep's droppings, and that the weight of the droppings was one index of the nutritive value of the herbage on which the flock had been feeding last. This flock was being put to graze on each of the strips of different herbage in turn, and the evidence of the bag would help the experts to decide which kind of herbage to select. Evidently agronomy is an exact science— at least, as agronomy is practised at Estanzuela.

The super-sheep-breeding station among the hills behind Punta del Este is a private enterprise. When I saw the rockiness of the terrain, I was surprised that this location should have been selected. The explanation was that these rocky hills provided a perennial supply of water, and that the irrigation of the meadows was the key to keeping the stock in prime condition. The leanness of the rough pasture was more than compensated for by the richness of the small patches of irrigated land. The inspiration of this super-sheep-breeding estancia had come from New Zealand, and the show-piece was a New Zealand ram. He was standing proudly in his pen, with a couple of Uruguayan rams attending on him, one on each side. The natives were proud to be in the company of the magnificent foreign immigrant, while the immigrant seemed to be taking their homage for granted. All three creatures were so highly bred that they seemed hardly—I was going to say 'human', but what I mean is 'hardly ovine' any longer.

Why should a place in a Spanish-speaking country be called Young? The name commemorates the enterprising-ness of a couple of Scots who, a century and more ago, made their way up the Uruguay River and saw that the country round the Uruguay's left-bank tributary, the Rio Negro, would be a splendid pastureland for cattle. They bought land cheap. (The site of Young was then on the northern frontier of settlement in Uruguay.) They stocked their land with Herefords, and their descendants were holding their annual cattle-sale on the day of my visit. During the morn-ing, the buyers were arriving, some on horseback, some in cars, and some in mini-planes that landed, like our Cessna plane, on the estancia's private airstrip. There were some keen buyers from Brazil and from Argentina. These had not made their long journeys for nothing; they knew just what they wanted and they went on bidding till they secured it. As for the general run of buyers, it was reckoned, so I was told, that they would bid more recklessly after the barbecue, washed down with strong drink, to which all comers were invited. This lavish hospitality was also good business.

The auctioneer was not a new figure for me; I had seen his counterparts in Cumberland and in Texas. The Hereford bulls were not new to me either. I had seen their equals in New South Wales. What interested me most was the Scottish-Argentinian family to whom the estancia and its livestock belonged. There were at least three, and perhaps four, generations of them present, and each successive generation was a perceptible degree more Argentinian than its immediate predecessor. I doubt whether any of the children spoke any English at all, and even the oldest of the ladies of the house spoke her English with a Spanish accent. I was watching a process of assimilation that was certainly voluntary and was probably unconscious. This once Scottish family was anchored irrevocably to its good Uruguayan land and to the magnificent cattle that the family was breeding on it. They might cease to be Scottish in all but name, but they would continue, generation after generation, to breed their Hereford bulls.

By the time when the Ministry of Agriculture's Cessna plane returned me to Montevideo, I felt that I had caught at least a glimpse of the rural sources of the city's livelihood.

The Pampa

My anticipatory mental picture of the Uruguayan campo had been vague; my picture of the Argentine pampa had been precise. I had imagined a dead flat stoneless green prairie stretching away and away to the horizon, with not one tree, house, or fence to break the continuity of the view. There are stretches of the pampa that still do look rather like that, when one is flying over them at an altitude that is high enough to flatten out the silhouettes of any objects that stand up above the surface. When one traverses the pampa nowadays by road, however, the effect is very different from the picture that I had imagined. This picture may have been more or less true to the reality of a hundred years ago, when the gauchos (Argentina's cowboys) were pasturing their herds on the open range, and when the pampa's coat of grass had not yet been torn open by the plough. Today the pampa is, of course, still dead flat and still stoneless, but in other respects its appearance has been transformed.

A large part of the pampa is now under cultivation. In September—which, in the Southern Hemisphere, is the beginning of spring—the fields are bare of crops, and the richness of the good dark soil is revealed. For a long time the Argentine pampa has been one of the World's principal sources of cereals. Rosario, which contests with Córdoba the claim to be the second largest city in the country, rose to greatness as a grain port, and 'Rosafé' wheat—shipped abroad from Rosario and from Santa Fé, higher up the

Paraná River—is much sought after in the world-market. Cultivation has brought settlement with it. On this fertile soil, the farms are of moderate size. On the pampa to the west of Buenos Aires, farm-buildings are sown thick over the landscape. Villages are frequent, and there are also large country towns, each surrounded by a ring of factories. In fact, the farmer, shopkeeper, and industrialist have taken effective possession of the pampa, and have expelled the gaucho from it into the shadowy realm of historical romance. Stock-breeding has now become a matter-of-fact business. On a present-day cattle-estancia a tractor-driver earns higher wages than a horseman. The pastures, as well as the arable lands, are now fenced. European breeds of cattle are being crossed with the Indian zebú in the hope of giving the cross-breed the zebú's immunity from the tick. A voluntary association of breeders has introduced artificial insemination.

The greatest surprise, for me, however, was the multitude of the trees. Every one of these has been planted by Man, except perhaps the willows; yet there are so many trees on the western pampa now that there are no distant views to be had there any longer. Almost every farm there now includes a plantation, and, on the cattle-estancias, there are wind-breaks of poplar or eucalyptus. The effect is like the land-scape of Normandy. In the climate of Normandy, though, a wind-break of trees will not do duty for a cow-byre. In the milder climate of Argentina and Uruguay, the trees give the cattle enough shelter to allow them, with impunity, to stay out in the open, night and day, in all seasons. At Young in north-western Uruguay, for instance, the precious Hereford bulls that I saw being sold at tall prices spend their nights, year in and year out, huddled in the hollow interior of a thicket planted for the purpose. The cattle industry in Uruguay and Argentina has been favoured by Nature. With the cattle living out in the open all the year round, the lay-out of the farm-buildings can be kept down to a minimum, and this, of course, keeps down the overhead costs of operation.

The western pampa's vast extent can no longer be seen with the eye; the intruding trees have screened off the former distant horizon; but the vastness can still be felt with all the bones and muscles in one's body when one travels over the pampa by car. The main roads have a good surface, but the distances are immense. If one drives out west-north-westwards from Buenos Aires, one is kept wondering, for the first hour, whether one is ever going to see the pampa at all. Has Buenos Aires swallowed up the pampa? Has it melted into Córdoba and Mendoza? Has it swept on beyond, to break, in a wave of streets and buildings, against the eastern flank of the Andes? Buenos Aires is going to do all that one day—and this not in a very remote future. Today, however, the pampa's immensity is still more than a match for Buenos Aires' expansive power, dynamic though this is. After the first hour's travelling along the west-north-westward roads, the 'zona urbanizada' peters out, and the fields and farms have the country to themselves. While one is still within the bounds of Buenos Aires province, one crosses occasional small streams, fringed with willows, that are winding their way across the pampa to join the Paraná River. The last of these is the one that flows through the country town of Pergamíno. There are no streams in the southern tip of the province of Santa Fé, and none in the south-east corner of the province of Córdoba, but the pampa is not here perceptibly losing its greenness. After crossing the boundary between Santa Fé and Córdoba, we turn off the high road north-north-eastwards to visit a cattle-estancia near the village of Cavanagh. (On the pampa, Irish place-names are frequent.) We have been travelling now for the best part of five hours; our bones and muscles are our built-in chronometers; but, in this direction, the end of the green pampa is not yet in sight.

'How far does the pampa extend beyond here?' we ask our hosts on this estancia in the corner of Córdoba province. 'Oh, about as far as the distance that you have covered on your way to here from Buenos Aires.' A glance at the map shows that this estimate is not an exaggeration. However, the pampa, as well as Buenos Aires, does have an end. It ends quite abruptly on the route that we followed when, a few days later, we flew from Buenos Aires to the north-western city of Salta. This air-route runs to the north-east of the road to Cavanagh. It follows the course of the Paraná River up to, and over, Rosario. After that the air-route sheers away north-westwards from the river, while the pattern of fields below the plane runs on and on. Is the pampa interminable? As one starts to wonder about this, one suddenly sees the last row of fields break off against the white shore of a salt lake, the Mar Chiquita (Little Sea). Will the fields begin again beyond this lake's farther shore? The question is answered quickly and dramatically. The country beyond is naked desert, and the desert stretches on until, as we are fastening our seat-belts for the descent to Salta, we see rise up, on our left front, a line of mountains that is the eastern-most range of the Andes. The distance from the Little Sea to Salta is greater than the distance from Buenos Aires to the Little Sea. The pampa, which has outrun Buenos Aires city, has been outdistanced, in its turn, by the north-western desert.

The Argentine pampa reminds the traveller of Illinois and Iowa; the north-western desert reminds him of Colorado or, more exactly, of the Middle East of the Old World. Yet the desert, too, can support a surprising amount of life. Kilgru-men, the estancia near Cavanagh that we visited, is associated with another in the arid north-west. The north-west breeds the cattle; Kilgrumen takes them over to be fattened for the Buenos Aires market. Here, as at Estanzuela and Young in Uruguay, we came to close quarters with the livestock, and were astonished to find how tame they are in La Plata compared to the cattle and sheep of Europe. In La Plata, bulls are handled in as off-hand a way as if they were mere cows, yet they show no inclination to bellow or gore. Latin America seems to have solved the problem of race relations, not only between different breeds of Man, but also between Man and his domesticated animals.

There are different ways of taking the pampa's measure. One can measure it by its extent; alternatively, one can measure it by its productivity. When we repeated our five-hours' drive on the return journey from Cavanagh to Buenos Aires on a Sunday evening, we found ourselves caught up into an endless procession of great lorries. These were carrying the produce of the pampa to Buenos Aires, to unload it there in time for the Monday morning market. The pampa may not be interminable; the desert may beat the pampa in sheer extent; yet the pampa is big enough to account for the size of Buenos Aires. Like its smaller sister Montevideo, Buenos Aires is a parasite on its rural hinterland.

Both the fertility and the immensity of the pampa redoubled the first impression that they had made on us in the west when we made another five-hours' expedition from Buenos Aires—this time southward to Mar de Plata. We now discovered that Man's re-making of the pampa has taken different forms in different quarters. Along the southern road the pampa's local aspect was less unlike my anticipatory picture than it had been on our journey towards the west. Southward, ploughed fields and trees were rarer, horizons were more distant, streams and even rivers abounded. Indeed, the country here is so well-watered that it has had to be drained artificially by canals. This section of the pampa seemed to be given over almost entirely to lush green pastures. Yet, en route to Mar de Plata, we passed a large factory for the extraction of vegetable oil, so sunflower and other oil-producing crops must co-exist with pastures in this predominantly pastoral region. The land is so vast that, even if the cultivated patches are too small and too rare to be noticeable, their aggregate product will add up to a quantity sufficient to keep a large factory busy.

Between Mar de Plata and the port of Quequén, we had another surprise. Here pastures were as rare as arable had been on the pampa between Mar de Plata and Buenos Aires. Here, almost the whole of the pampa's bountiful black soil was under cultivation; so we were not surprised, at Quequén, to see two Greek ships—one registered at Peiraeus and the other at Ithaca—taking on board a cargo of grain from a giant elevator. In the town there was a Greek restaurant and a Greek tailor's shop, with their titles written up in the Greek language and alphabet. At Quequén, unexpectedly, I was finding part of the answer to the puzzling question of how the city of Athens manages to feed itself. But what does Greece export to Argentina in return for taking Argentina's cereals?

At Quequén we had to turn back, for Quequén is more than three hundred and fifty miles south of Buenos Aires as the road runs, and we had to be back in Buenos Aires that night. Once again, we had travelled till our bones ached without coming anywhere near to the end of the fertile pampa. Another two hundred and fifty miles would have brought us to Bahía Blanca, a grain-port on a scale that would have made the installations at Quequén look insignificant. What distances! What agricultural and pastoral wealth! The original handful of Spanish settlers at Buenos Aires staked out a fabulous heritage for their successors. It has required just about four centuries for the Argentine people to take possession of this heirloom of theirs. On the southern pampa, the work has all been done within my life-time. In 1889, the southern pampa was still Indian country. Gazing up at the sky-scraping apartment houses of Mar de Plata and the giant elevator at Quequén, I found myself feeling very old, when I recollected that all this apparatus had been called into existence since the year in which I was born.

The Paraná River

THE River Plate is the child of a marriage between the Uruguay and Paraná Rivers. These two rivers' combined discharge is so huge that the River Plate, too, is a fresh-water river, even as far out towards the Atlantic as Monte-video. At Montevideo, people are careful to call the waters that stretch away to the horizon 'the river', not 'the sea'. There is politics in this choice of words. If the waters off Montevideo were the sea, Uruguay's jurisdiction over them might be confined to a five-mile, or, at most, to a twelve-mile, limit. Since, however, the waters here are still fresh, not salt, they may fairly be called 'the river', and, if they are still a river at the point where they flow past Montevideo, then the whole of their breadth at this point—and here they are perhaps rather more than one hundred miles broad—can be claimed as Uruguayan and Argentinian territorial waters. The two republics' areas of jurisdiction will meet in the River Plate's talweg, leaving no cranny, in between, for a free sea. Paraguay may claim that the Paraná is an inter-national river, but Argentina will continue to turn a deaf ear to this claim, and Uruguay will take no interest in it, since her half of the breadth of the River Plate and of the Uruguay River give her as much navigable river-water of her own as she needs.

The Uruguay River would count as a long one if it were not outdistanced by the Paraná. The Paraná rises just to the south of Brasília and discharges into the River Plate just to the north of Buenos Aires. It would count as a long river if it were not outdistanced by the Amazon. The Amazon is the queen of all the rivers in the Americas in point of length. In this, it beats not only the Paraná but the Mississippi and the St. Lawrence (even if one reckons that the St. Lawrence rises at the head of Lake Superior). Only the greatest rivers of Africa and Asia can put the Amazon out of countenance.

Everyone knows about the Amazon; probably fewer people know about the Paraná; and this is partly the Paraná's own fault; for this great river has a sly way of concealing its size. If you were sailing up-stream on the River Plate, you might imagine that this was just the estuary of the Uruguay River, and you might enter the Uruguay River and follow it up, without realizing that the swamps which you had by-passed on your left bow concealed the delta of another river that is much greater than the Uruguay River is.

The Uruguay River makes the most of its waters by pouring them all down one single broad channel. The Paraná River, from its delta to a point up-stream above Rosario, does its utmost to conceal its volume by distributing its mighty waters among a host of separate channels. Seen from the air on a clear sunny day, this lowest section of the Paraná River's long course looks like a living belt plaited out of the writhing bodies of half-a-dozen silver-skinned snakes. The arms of the lower Paraná River part and rejoin and part again and weave their way in and out of each other as they go. From the air, even the broadest of these arms looks narrow. The south-westernmost arm, which flows out into the River Plate the nearest of all the arms to Buenos Aires, is a relatively minor channel; yet it too carries ocean-going ships, and, on a European, it makes the effect of being a giant river when he travels on its waters. The south-west bank of this arm is studded with a series of port-cities: Las

Conchas, Campana, Zarate, Baradero; but the major west-bank port is Rosario, higher up-stream. At Rosario the broadest arm of the Paraná washes up against a line of bluffs, which rise high above the highest flood-level. On the pampa, even modest heights are rarities; and heights that immediately overhang the Paraná River's broadest arm were predestined to become the site of a big port-city, as soon as the pampa had been turned into pastures and wheat-fields by settlers from Europe.

Where is Argentina's Litoral? One would expect the name to designate Argentina's enormously long Atlantic coast—a salt-water litoral that starts on the Argentine side of the estuary of the River Plate and runs from there all the way to Cape Horn. Actually the Litoral is the west bank of the lower Paraná River, and the nearest salt water is two hundred miles and more away from this Litoral's south-eastern end. The University of the Litoral has its head-quarters in Rosario, with a subsidiary centre farther up-stream at Santa Fé. (Though Santa Fé is the capital of the province that bears its name, Rosario is this province's biggest city.)

At Rosario I have seen the Paraná River from the bank; I have also seen it from the air; but I have sailed only on its relatively minor south-western branch. To reach this, we had to travel by road to the northern extremity of Buenos Aires city and then to embark on a launch on the River Tigré—a really small river that enters the River Plate independently, just to the south of the Paraná delta. From the Tigré River to the nearest arm of the Paraná, the launch had to thread its way through a maze of narrow waterways. The patches of dry land between these have been drained and been planted with citrus fruit, and each planta-tion is protected against foul weather by lines of eucalyptus or poplar which enclose it in a hollow square. The regularity

III Brazil: Olinda

IV Chile: the Andes overhanging Santiago

of the lay-out of these groves provides a pleasant foil for the waywardness of the encompassing backwaters. The traffic here is all water-borne, and this aquatic fruit-garden and playground of Buenos Aires can contest with the floating gardens of Mexico City the claim to be Latin America's Bangkok.

The waterways that intersect the citrus-groves of the Paraná delta twist and turn and appear to be leading nowhere, till suddenly one finds oneself shooting out into the south-westernmost channel of the lower Paraná. As one traverses its waters and notes the size of the commercial shipping that plies here, it is hard to realize that there are at least two larger channels farther to the north-east. It is also hard to realize that this water on which one is floating in the southern temperate zone has come all the way from the tropical highlands of Central Brazil and South-Eastern Bolivia, and that the Paraguay River, which joins the Paraná far, far up-stream, at Corrientes, is a tributary that can compare in magnitude with the Paraná itself. Yet the length of the Paraná River is only about one quarter of the length of the South American continent.

In all but a tiny fraction of this huge mass of land, the Spanish and Portuguese languages are current today. One or other of these languages has become the mother-tongue of the descendants of the immigrants who have flocked into South America from Italy and Germany and Poland and Syria and Japan. By the time when the present population explosion comes to a halt, Spanish and Portuguese will be spoken by perhaps four or five hundred million people in South America alone. The original handful of Portuguese settlers and Spanish conquistadores would have been astonished if they could have foreseen this consequence of their incursion into the New World.

E

Argentina's Two Worlds

IN Buenos Aires one is in the New World—the world of New York and Montreal and Sydney. This New World has been called into existence by settlers from Europe. In the act of pulling up their European roots and re-planting themselves overseas, these settlers have, of course, undergone a sea-change. These transmarine extensions of Europe are not exact reproductions of their European motherland. The new Europe overseas has developed a distinct character of its own. All the same, both the population and the civilization of this overseas European world are of wholly European origin. The former native inhabitants of these lands were still in a primitive stage of culture at the time when the European settlers impinged on them and overwhelmed them. They count for little or nothing in these countries' present-day life. The case is very different, however, in those countries in which the pre-Columbian inhabitants were cultivators of the soil, were planted thick on the ground, and had developed high civilizations of their own. When these civilized pre-Columbian peoples were subjugated by the conquistadores, they were submerged, but they survived, and, in Mexico and Bolivia, they have recently re-emerged. What happened in these two 'Indian-American' countries yesterday might happen tomorrow in Ecuador and Peru and also in North-Western Argentina.

When you fly, today, from Buenos Aires to Salta, you pass out of the New World back into the Old World at the point where the green pampa gives way to the brown and yellow desert. When a European crosses this line, his sensations are curious. The green landscape that he is now leaving behind him is much more like his own European homeland than is the desert that he is now entering; but simultaneously the European is re-entering the Old World; so, for him, the exoticness of the Northern Argentine landscape is counterbalanced by something familiar in the local culture.

In crossing this physiographical and cultural divide, the traveller from Buenos Aires is entering one of the provinces of the pre-Columbian civilization of the Andes; he is entering the former domain of the Inca Empire; and he is entering the section of the Viceroyalty of Buenos Aires that, after the Spanish conquest, was colonized by Spanish settlers via Panamá and Peru and not via the South Atlantic and the River Plate.

It is not surprising that the Andean civilization should have extended into what is now North-Western Argentina. This civilization was Man's answer to the challenge of a hard country—barren desert and bleak altoplano—and this kind of country extends from Peru through Bolivia into the present-day Argentine provinces of Jujúy and Salta and Catamarca and Santiago del Estero. The whole domain of the Andean culture was eventually incorporated politically in the Inca Empire; but the Incas did not push on, in any direction, very far beyond the Andean civilization's bounds. The primitive inhabitants of the outer darkness were not worth conquering or were too recalcitrant. Moreover, the expansion of the Inca Empire was limited by the unadaptability of the llama, which was the Incas' only means of transport besides their own feet. A llama begins to wilt if he is brought down much below an altitude of about one thousand metres. The Incas did annex and hold the Pacific seaboard of Peru; and, south-eastwards, they pushed on beyond the highlands of Salta to the plains of Santiago del Estero and Tucumán. But they could not advance farther than that beyond the llama's limit; and so, in Argentina, they came to a halt, like the Norse settlers in Greenland, just when they had reached the verge of a potentially rich land. The Greenlanders never established themselves in Vinland; the Incas never occupied the Argentine pampa.

When the Spaniards overthrew the Inca Empire and seized its domain, they were more enterprising. The Spaniards did push on from the oasis of Tucumán across the desert of Santiago del Estero to the oasis of Córdoba, and from there they felt their way across the pampa to the west bank of the Paraná River and descended this waterway to its debouchure into the River Plate. Buenos Aires, as well as Córdoba, was founded before the close of the sixteenth century, and the corridor between Pacific and Atlantic that had thus been opened up was never lost. Córdoba, however, was the farthest point south that was colonized from Peru and that represented the Peruvian variety of overseas Spanish culture. The route from Spain to Buenos Aires via Panamá and Lima and the Peruvian-Bolivian altoplano was too roundabout and too laborious, considering that the River Plate could be reached so much more easily and quickly from Spain via the South Atlantic. Thus, while Córdoba continued to look towards Lima, Buenos Aires came to look towards Europe. Somewhere on the pampa between Córdoba and the Paraná River the two streams of settlement and two varieties of Spanish culture met.

They met, and their representatives eventually worked together against the Spanish Crown in the war of independence. Yet, though they met, they never fused with each other completely. The present-day tension between Córdoba and Buenos Aires is an indication that Argentina is a meeting-place between two worlds. At the time of the war of independence, Córdoba was already an important city, while Buenos Aires was then still an insignificant little port. In the course of the next century and a half, Buenos Aires left Córdoba far behind. While Córdoba continued to sleep a Peruvian-like slumber, Buenos Aires built herself up into a great modern city by importing European immigrants on a North American scale to populate her vast hinterland on the pampa and to develop its potential wealth. Córdoba was piqued but remained torpid, till suddenly, within the last few years, this once old-fashioned city began to transform herself into an industrial centre. This is Córdoba's retort to Buenos Aires. The retort is belated. Córdoba will surely never catch up with Buenos Aires till, in the coming age of the world-city, Ecumenopolis, these two rivals melt into one after expanding to meet each other across the breadth of the pampa.

The rivalry between Córdoba and Buenos Aires has now been translated into terms of modern technology. Yet the contrast, that this rivalry symbolizes, between the north and the south of Argentina dates from pre-Columbian times. It is the contrast between the Andean civilization and the barbarism beyond its southern bounds. It is also the contrast between the Inca Empire and the untamed Indians beyond its southern frontier. The cleft between present-day Argentina's two worlds is thus an ancient one. It will not be obliterated till the coming world-city has fused these two worlds together by submerging them both under a continuous lava-flow of urban streets and houses.

Salta and Beyond

TODAY, Salta is the terminus of a Caravelle-flight from Buenos Aires which covers the distance in one hour and forty minutes in the air. Before the arrival of the railway age, Salta was the terminus of a horse-route from Buenos Aires which required many, many days in the saddle. For the horse, as for the Caravelle, Salta was the end. A horse could not make its way from Salta on to the altoplano and over the Andes. So, at Salta, the traveller from Buenos Aires to Lima had to sell his horse and buy a mule, while the traveller from Lima to Buenos Aires would sell his mule at Salta and buy a horse, to do the rest of his journey by the speediest means of conveyance then available. This was good for Salta. The city became a flourishing horse and mule market.

From Salta the next staging-point on the journey to Lima is Jujúy. This city stands on the bank of one of Spanish America's innumerable Rio Grandes. Salta stands on the bank of a tributary of the same river, and, by making a detour, it is possible to travel from Salta to Jujúy on the flat. The railway was the first form of modern transportation to do this; the present-day motor-road has imitated the railway. A mechanized means of conveyance will be happy to lengthen its route to any degree for the sake of avoiding a gradient. But that has not been the policy of men and mules. These have always preferred the shortest route, however steep. The direct route from Salta to Jujúy climbs over a mountain; and this was the route that pedestrians and muleteers took as a matter of course in the days of the Spanish Empire of the Indies. No doubt they were following in the footsteps of the Incas and of the Incas' predecessors during many previous centuries. The route that is technically the best for an engine-driver or a chauffeur is, of course, always the worst for a traveller whose object in travelling is to see the World, so it was fortunate for me that the provincial authorities of Salta and Jujúy have not let the old road between the two cities go to wrack and ruin. This old road, which was the attractive road for me, has been made practicable for motor-traffic. It climbs, twisting and turning, along the mountain-side through a forest that has a less tropical air than the forest in the hinterland of São Paulo, though Jujúy province is in the same latitude as São Paulo city and Itú.

From Jujúy the valley of the Rio Grande climbs due northward towards Bolivia. The road and railway from Buenos Aires to La Paz ascend this valley side by side, and here the traveller has no choice between better routes and worse; a wall of mountains hems the valley in on either side; so, on this section of the long haul, everyone must travel by one route only—the valley route—if he is to travel at all. Going up by car, we were not conscious of the steepness of the gradient, but we inferred it from the behaviour of the international train that we overtook and quickly passed. The train was crawling, yet the engine was panting, and it was heading for a section of the permanent way on which it would have to lever itself up by rack and pinion; the gradient is here too steep to allow the train to climb without the aid of this crutch. In our car we ascended the valley for about one hundred miles, ate a leisurely lunch at Humahuaca, and, on the homeward journey, free-wheeling steeply down, we passed the same international train again. It was still panting, yet it had made no perceptible progress towards its goal.

The Incas followed this valley, like their Spanish supplanters and the Spanish muleteers' successors the British railway-engineers. The Incas came, saw, conquered, and consolidated their conquests by building fortresses and planting garrisons. About one-third of the way from Jujúy to Humahuaca there are the ruins of an Inca fortress on a spur of the eastern mountain-range that juts out westwards till it overhangs the river. The siting of this fortress bears witness to the sureness of the Incas' eye in singling out strategic positions. From the summit of the spur on which this particular Inca fortress was planted, one can see, not only far up and down the Rio Grande valley itself, but also right up a lateral valley on either side. There is said to be a sister fortress, still unexplored by archaeologists, on a corresponding spur of the valley's western mountain-barrier.

The Rio Grande valley above Jujúy is Indian country. In the nooks and crannies of the mountains there are Indians who are still leading a primitive life. In the Rio Grande valley itself and in its nearer and more accessible side-valleys, the Indians have learnt to speak Spanish and to wear clothes of the local Argentinian rural style, but this without being yet truly assimilated to the Argentinians of European race. An Argentinian lady who received us in her house at Jujúy had taken into her household two daughters of an Indian village woman who had made contact with the lady by asking her to serve as godmother for her latest baby. One girl had fitted well into modern life; the other had not.

On our way up the valley, we turned aside into a lateral valley to the west, in order to visit an Indian village. This Indian community's heritage was a barren one, measured by the standard of fertility that is set in Argentina by the pampa and by the northern oases. Yet the rugged little valley's Indian inhabitants had made the most of what Nature had given to them. Every patch of utilizable soil had

been either cultivated or been planted with fruit trees or
been laid down to pasture for a cow or for a couple of sheep.
What would these Indians make of a patrimony of the same
size in Buenos Aires province? Would they show the same
assiduity in turning it to the utmost account? Or would the
novel experience of affluence have the effect of relaxing the
efforts which their present penury evokes?

Humahuaca is not only an Indian name; it is also still
an Indian townlet. At Humahuaca the traveller is already
about seven thousand feet above sea level, and this is more
than half way, in altitude, between the city of Jujúy and the
twelve-thousand-feet-high Bolivian altoplano. As I stood at
the north end of the little town, and gazed up the road that
climbs on beyond it towards Bolivia, I longed to follow the
road farther. At Humahuaca one is within about one hundred
miles of the Argentine-Bolivian frontier. Ten years back,
at Juli on the south-west shore of Lake Titicáca, I had been
still nearer to Bolivia than that. I have now approached
Bolivia from two sides, but I have not yet set foot on
Bolivian soil; I have not yet set eyes on the temple at
Tiahuanaco.

As I was travelling up and down the Rio Grande valley,
I was feeling all the time that this was a familiar landscape.
I had never been here before. Where on earth was it that I
had previously travelled through a valley that looked like
this? Why, of course, it was in Afghanistan; and, as I
recognized the affinity between two lands that lie on opposite
sides of the globe, I ran into the work of someone who had
been before me in recognizing that the Rio Grande valley
was a piece of Afghanistan that had been transplanted to the
New World. This enterprising European—he was either a
Scot or a German—had not only recognized this; he had
acted on his intuition. He had bought land in the valley;
he had irrigated it; he had surrounded his irrigated fields

with wind-breaks of poplar and eucalyptus; and he had stocked the fields with karakol sheep. As we drove past the serried ranks of grey-green trees, past the fresh green pastures, and past the black flocks browsing on the rich grass, the illusion was complete. For a moment I was in the Bamian valley; and then, as we left the last pasture, flock, and wind-break behind, I was back in South America again.

Argentina's Northern Oases

ON the pampa, pasture and arable are continuous, and this unbroken expanse of productive soil is vast. Apply a pair of dividers to a map of South America; plant one of the two points in Buenos Aires city and the other in the city of Bahía Blanca. The direct distance between the two points will be approximately four hundred miles. Then, taking Buenos Aires as your centre-point, describe the circumference of a circle with a four-hundred-miles-long radius, starting at Bahía Blanca and running from there first north-westwards, then northwards, then eastwards. The line will hit the Argentine-Brazilian frontier on the Uruguay River about fifty miles above the meeting-point of the frontiers of Argentina, Brazil, and Uruguay. It will fall short of Córdoba, but it will pass through 'the Little Sea' (the Mar Chiquita). The whole of the area enclosed by this line is fertile pampa, but, beyond the line, conditions are dramatically different. Beyond the line, the desert is the rule, and the patches of cultivation and pastureland are the exceptions.

Nature, who has been so bountiful to Man inside that magic circle, has been niggardly to him outside it. What has she withheld? Not the chemical constituents that make the soil potentially fertile, but the water without which this potential fertility cannot fructify. The productive areas in the North-West of Argentina, beyond the pampa, are isolated oases in which sufficient water does reach the soil, either in rainfall or in perennial rivers or by means of irrigation, where rain-water or river-water can be stored in reservoirs. The principal north-western oases, in their order from south to north, are those that support the cities of Córdoba, Tucumán, Salta, and Jujúy, and all four have the same physical setting. All four are open to the east, but have, just to the west of them, a north-south chain of mountains. In consequence, the rain-bearing clouds, travelling westward from the Atlantic, precipitate their waters at the mountains' eastern foot. The oases are thus assured of rain-water, however capricious the clouds may be in choosing their times and seasons; and, if the mountain valleys are converted into reservoirs by the building of barrages, the rain that falls on the mountains themselves can be stored there for distribution all round the year. The water from the reservoirs can be used for generating hydro-electric power, as well as for irrigation, and the hydro-electric potentialities of the Sierra de Córdoba are one of the inducements that have led important industries—for instance Industrias Kaiser Argentina— to establish branches at Córdoba within the last few years.

The effect of the westerly range of mountains in making the clouds discharge is illustrated by the contrast between the oasis of Tucumán and the desert of Santiago del Estero. Santiago lies only about one hundred miles to the south-east of Tucumán, but that addition to the distance from the western mountains is enough to make the clouds sail over Santiago, reserving their gift of rain till they reach Tucumán. In consequence, Santiago del Estero state is as bare as a bone, while Tucumán state is a sea of sugar-cane plantations.

As far south as Tucumán inclusive, the oases of what is now North-Western Argentina were occupied by a civilized sedentary Indian population in the pre-Columbian Age. This region was an outlying province of the domain of the civilization of the Andes, and, like the rest of the Andean World, it was eventually incorporated in the Inca Empire. After the Inca Empire, and the Andean civilization with it, had been destroyed by the Spanish conquistadores, the country's economy was built up again, from the foundations, by the Jesuits. They gathered the Indians together under their wing in *reducciones* (settlements), and taught them Western arts, not only the Western style of agriculture and animal husbandry, but Western industrial arts as well. In the foothills of the Sierra de Córdoba I visited the Jesuit church of Santa Catalina, which passed into private possession after the dissolution of the Society of Jesus in the seventeen-sixties. Happily this church has been restored, and is being kept in repair, by four families that are its present owners. Among the sugar-plantations in the Tucumán oasis, on the road from Tucumán to Concepción, I visited a Jesuit church that has been allowed to fall into ruins. It was the church of the congregation of Jesuits that introduced the cultivation of sugar into Tucumán. When the Society was dissolved, sugar-cultivation in Tucumán disappeared with it. It was revived in the nineteenth century, and its subsequent success is Tucumán's present economic problem.

Its success was so great that the Tucumán oasis became a single-crop country. This is dangerous everywhere and always, and in Tucumán today it is disastrous. Tucumán's sugar industry has been running at a loss for a long time now. Tucumán's two rivals to the north, Salta and Jujúy, manage to extract twice as much sugar as Tucumán from an equal amount of cane. Neither the province nor the country as a whole can carry this lame-dog industry for ever. Tucumán's agriculture ought to be diversified again, and the most promising substitute for sugar here is citrus fruit. A start has been made in bringing about the change; but this economic-ally necessary agricultural revolution raises a financial and a social problem, and both problems are formidable.

If sugar-cane plantations are to be replaced by citrus groves, the roots of the cane have to be extracted from the soil, and this is a laborious and costly operation. After that, when the soil has been made fit for planting with citrus trees, the new crop will produce no fruit for the first five, or perhaps even seven, years. How is a landowner to meet the initial expense and the subsequent loss of income? He is not an inviting applicant for a loan on a commercial basis. Nothing short of massive financial aid, on easy terms, from the Argentine Government or the World Bank or the Alliance for Progress can make it possible for Tucumán to extricate itself from sugar and to replace this by a crop that promises, in the end, to bring in an economic return. In any case, the capital sunk in the milling machinery will have to be written off as a dead loss. This machinery is massive, complex, expensive, and highly specialized. It will only mill sugar; it cannot be put to work on any other job.

The social problem is the unemployment that the liquidation of the sugar industry is bound to bring with it. The work, both in the fields and in the mills, is seasonal. The harvesting requires so many hands while it lasts that temporary workers have to be brought in from Bolivia, though, for the greater part of the year, the permanent agricultural population of Tucumán suffers severely from unemployment. Yet, even allowing for this, the sugar industry employs more hands for more of the time than are likely to be employed by anything that may replace it. So, for Tucumán, economic reform spells social trouble. In these circumstances it is not surprising that mill-owners and landowners and mill-hands and field-hands should be presenting a solid front against proposals for economic change. What they are asking is, in effect, that they should continue to operate an uneconomic industry at their fellow-countrymen's expense. This may be human, but it is not reasonable and it is not practical either. One thing is certain: Tucumán cannot stay as she is.

Falklands or Malvinas?

I HAPPENED to be in Argentina, at Córdoba, at the moment when the 'commando' forced the captive Argentinian plane to land in the Falklands, and when the news of this melodramatic performance was followed by the news of the attacks on the British embassy in Buenos Aires and on the British consulate in Rosario. As was to be expected, both the Argentine and the British Government have behaved with exemplary prudence and—what is even more important —with mutual understanding and good will. The Argentine Government's anger at the misbehaviour of a handful of youthful Argentine citizens was natural enough. Under the cloak of pretendedly patriotic gestures, the participants in the 'commando' escapade and the more serious offenders who fired the shots were actually seeking to embarrass their own Government, at the possible cost of sabotaging its attempt to arrive at an agreed settlement of the long-standing dispute over the islands. The saboteurs' action was therefore severely censured, not only by the Government, but by the responsible newspapers. However, we in Britain should note that, in censuring the wrongheadedness of the offenders' 'direct action', both the press and the Government also took pains to emphasize the point that all Argentinians are agreed in maintaining that the islands are lawfully theirs, that the British claim to them is invalid, and that the British occupation of them is consequently an illegitimate usurpation. In this the Argentine Government and people are unanimous, and this is not just an academic stand; the issue with Britain over the islands arouses deep and passionate feelings in Argentine hearts.

This psychological fact is unquestionable, and its political importance is obvious, but the cause of it is not self-evident. Why does the issue over the political status of these islands excite emotion on the Argentine side? The economic and strategic value of the islands is virtually nil, and they are remote from the Argentinian mainland, even in terms of the Argentinian scale of distances. The islands of St. Pierre and Miquelon lie much closer to Canada, and the Channel Islands much closer to France, yet the French and the Canadians do not react in the emotional Argentinian way to the presence of foreign flags on islands that are so much nearer to their coasts than the Falklands are to the nearest point in Continental Argentina.

The clue to this psychological puzzle may lie in a difference of psychological atmosphere which struck me when I passed into Argentina out of Brazil. These two Latin American peoples take their nationalism in a very different spirit from each other. Nationalism is, of course, an ideology that is to be found in every one of the 125 sovereign independent local states on the face of this planet, but the local strength of nationalism varies greatly from country to country, and, on this point, the contrast is particularly piquant as between the two biggest countries in Latin America. The Brazilians' nationalism is ironic and light-hearted; the Argentinians' nationalism is romantic and intense. What is the origin of this difference of emotional attitude? In part, maybe, it goes back to some difference between the Castilian and the Portuguese tradition, but I believe the main cause is the difference in the circumstances in which these two American countries parted company politically with their parent countries in Europe.

The Brazilians are fortunate in having parted company with Portugal peacefully. Actually, it was Portugal that had to disentangle herself from Brazil, not Brazil from Portugal; and Brazil let Portugal secede without bloodshed. Consequently it would be difficult, either in Portugal or in Brazil, to manufacture hero-liberators and to pose them on horseback in bronze, dressed in the uniforms of early-nineteenth-century general officers. Unfortunately for Argentina and for Spain, their parting, like the parting between the United States and Britain, cost a war; and the Argentine war of liberation has left an abiding mark on the Argentinian people's national consciousness and national feeling. Look at the battle-pictures in the national museum at Buenos Aires; visit the shrine of San Martín in Buenos Aires cathedral, and the other shrine that has been made out of the house in Tucumán in which the first Argentinian national assembly promulgated its declaration of independence. Then you will begin to understand the intensity of Argentine feelings about the Malvinas, as the contested islands are called in Argentine parlance.

Every Argentinian feels genuine pain at the thought that the British flag flies over the islands. Few people in Britain would feel any comparable pain if the Argentine flag were to fly there instead. On the principle of 'the greatest happiness of the greatest number', this is an argument for a transfer of the sovereignty over the islands. There is, however, a small number of people whose happiness is at stake to a far higher degree than the happiness of the inhabitants of the Argentine mainland and Britain. These are the actual inhabitants of the islands. If the islands do change hands, this will make no difference to the personal lives of either the people of Argentina or the people of Britain. On the other hand, the personal lives of the islanders will be deeply affected. This is the human aspect of the Falklands, alias

F

Malvinas, question; and both the Argentine and the British people owe it to the islanders, as their fellow human beings, to make sure that the islanders do not suffer as a result of any change of sovereignty. This should not be difficult; there are only about 2,000 islanders; and there are a number of alternative options that could be offered to them. But their human rights must be secured, and this is a condition to which any settlement of the political question must be subject.

Mendoza

MENDOZA was the last place in Argentina that I visited, but it was one of the first pieces of the country that I had come to know. A traveller cannot spend many hours in Argentina without drinking one or more of Mendoza's wines. These wines are of many varieties, and, so far as I have sampled them, every variety is good. The wines of Mendoza are drunk all over Argentina. They deserve to be drunk all over the World. They could confidently compete with the wines of Latin Europe and the Rhineland. The handicap that confines the market for them to Argentina itself is not any intrinsic inferiority; it is the present state of Argentina's ailing economy. This makes the foreign market unprofitable; and, in spite of Argentina's present economic troubles, the home market for Mendoza's wines is buoyant enough to make the Mendoza oasis one of the most prosperous regions of Argentina today.

Draw a straight line on the map between Buenos Aires and Santiago, and you will find Mendoza slightly to the north of this. In terms of distance, Mendoza is far from Buenos Aires; the whole breadth of the pampa, at its broadest, lies between, with a considerable stretch of western desert added to that. By comparison, the distance from Mendoza to Santiago is trifling; and, in fact, the plane, whose pace is not governed by the configuration of the Earth's surface, does the trip from Mendoza to Santiago in forty minutes, while the flight from Buenos Aires to

Mendoza is a matter of hours. The air time-table, however, is deceptive; for that forty minutes' flight carries the traveller over the Andes, and this is at least a day's journey by train or car, and a twenty-one days' journey for the cattle that cross the mountains from Chile to Argentina on the hoof to be fattened on the pampa. The passage across the Andes between Mendoza and Chile is arduous; yet in the pre-Columbian age, when the only means of conveyance was men's and llamas' feet, it was easier to reach the Mendoza oasis from the west, across the mountains, than from the east, across the desert. The art of agriculture, and the other arts of civilization that went with it, came to the Mendoza oasis, through the Andes, from Chile; the Incas subsequently extended their empire to Mendoza by the same route; and the Spaniards followed at the Incas' heels. The city of Mendoza, and the river of the same name which provides the oasis with most of its water for irrigation, are named after the leader of the first band of Spanish pioneers. The mountain-route between the central valley of Chile and the Mendoza oasis follows the course of the Mendoza river on the eastern side of the watershed.

Nowadays, this route is traversed by a narrow-gauge railway—built by British engineers—and by a motor-road as well. From Mendoza we followed this road, up into the mountains, to within forty miles of the present Argentine-Chilean frontier. The valley narrows and widens and narrows again as road and railway push their way upwards through a series of ranges which rise in height as one mounts westward. I longed to go over the top, but this was October, and the pass is not open for motor-traffic till December (the equivalent of the Northern Hemisphere's June). We could have taken the train, which burrows under the summit and is therefore able to run at all seasons. I had been eager to do this railway-journey; for, in the past, I had heard ecstatic accounts of the beauty of the scenery from travellers who had made the trip. We were gently but firmly deflected from the train to the plane, and I submitted to this kind shepherding with a bad grace. I felt sure that, in the plane, I should, as usual, see nothing but the upper surfaces of the clouds. However, fortune was kind to us. On the afternoon on which we flew over this section of the Andes, there was not a cloud in the sky, and the parallel ranks of glistening ranges stretched away to the horizon, north and south. In Santiago, two days later, I met an unfortunate man who was just back from meeting a party of travellers that had insisted on taking the train. They had arrived at the Chilean terminus of the Andes Railway at two o'clock in the morning, five hours behind the scheduled time; so, what with the darkness of night and the darkness of the tunnels, they cannot have seen any more of the Andes than one would see from the plane on a normal cloudy day.

If, instead of following the Mendoza River up into the mountains, you go to meet it at the point where it drops down into the plain, you will find yourself at the head of the works that give the Mendoza oasis its life. These works are a barrage that diverts the river's flow from its shingle bed to the main irrigation canal and the branch canals that distribute these life-giving waters. The irrigation-water is carried by force of gravity, and it is carried far. The Mendoza oasis is about 110 miles long from south to north and about 90 miles broad from west to east. Ninety per cent. of this area is irrigated by river water, and only 10 per cent. by wells; and, of the 90 per cent. that is supplied by four rivers, the greater part is the Mendoza River's contribution.

The Mendoza oasis is a world apart from Eastern Argentina. The pampa is akin to the North European plain; but, when you have left the pampa behind and have skimmed over the insulating western desert, you find yourself in a landscape that you would take for a piece of Syria or Iran if you could forget that you were now in the New World. The trees, and the runnels that keep the trees alive, remind you of Damascus and Isfahan. In the Mendoza oasis, too, both the city-streets and the country-roads are flanked by avenues of over-arching trees that give every thoroughfare the aspect of a never-ending bower. Here, too, you find double lines of poplars bathing their roots in a rivulet that flows between them; and, here too, avenue and rivulet are as regularly aligned as a regiment of eighteenth-century soldiers.

Out in the oasis, the avenues and rivulets embrace the vineyards. We visited one bodega that ran to more than 1,800 acres of irrigated vine-land—a fantastically valuable estate. This bodega produces thirty-two different varieties of wine, every one of them a *grand vin* in the French sense. Here the whole immensely skilful and painstaking process of production is inspired by French models. Even the huge barrels in which the wines mature are made of imported French oak.

I have noted already that Mendoza's wine industry works for the Argentinian home market, not for export. Today the rest of Argentina, like most of the rest of the World, is in a state of simmering unrest. The atmosphere in Mendoza is an exception to this general rule. For instance, the local university is singular among the state universities of Argentina in being immune, so far, from student strikes. If a luxury industry, such as the Mendoza wine industry is, can support an apparently contented community on the scale of the dense population of the Mendoza oasis, the rest of Argentina, on whose patronage Mendoza depends, cannot really be so badly off as the present state of Argentina's economy and finances suggests. On the surface, life in Argentina is difficult today; yet this uneasy surface is underpinned by the country's vast natural resources. A large part—perhaps the greater part—of these resources is still untapped. However uncomfortable the present time in Argentina may be, the country's future is surely secure.

An Aperçu of Chile

THE eighteen successor-states of the former Spanish Empire of the Indies have all inherited the Spanish language from their common political past, yet this is their only common legacy from Spain that seems likely to endure. Of the Spanish-speaking overseas countries, like the English-speaking overseas countries, each has been developing a national ethos of its own. In the cultural make-up of each Spanish-speaking country there is, of course, a residual Spanish element, but the strength of this ancestral heritage differs appreciably from country to country.

In Argentina a strong flavour of Spanish ceremoniousness still survives, and this is a paradox; for Argentina is more assiduous than any other Spanish-American country in keeping alive the memory of its war of independence against the Spanish Crown, and Argentina has also diluted its population's original Spanish stock with a larger infusion of non-Spanish European blood than any other Spanish-American country so far. All the same, Argentina's abiding Spanishness is borne in on the traveller when he hops over the Andes from Argentina to Chile; for here, in this former Spanish captain-generalcy, the atmosphere is now strikingly different from what it is in the former Spanish viceroyalty of Buenos Aires. The difference is, indeed, so marked that one guesses that it must date from well before the achievement of independence a century and a half ago.

Though Argentina has been a republic for this length of

time, her official life still retains much of the formality of
the eighteenth-century European monarchical régime. The
official residences of Argentinian provincial governors are
palatial, and some of these palaces have been built within the
last sixty or seventy years. By contrast, official life in Chile is
less stiff. Even the President's palace in Santiago is relatively
modest. (It is distinguished, not by its scale, but by the
elegance of its architecture.) President Frei and his ministers
behave like ordinary mortals. They behave, in fact, as their
counterparts behave in the United States and Canada and
Australia and New Zealand. Chilean statesmen are approach-
able—the more so because, under the present régime, their
average age is young for men occupying the highest positions
of public responsibility—and, in this attractive feature, the
members of the present Chilean Government are, I should
say, fair samples of the Chilean people as a whole. Chileans
do not stand on ceremony, and they have a sense of humour
which they share with the Brazilians, unlike though they are
to these in most other respects.

In its racial make-up, Chile resembles Argentina and
Uruguay in being predominantly European, but this perhaps not quite to the same degree. In Chile, as in Argentina,
there are still some unassimilated or imperfectly assimilated
Indians in regions remote from the capital. In Argentina you
find them in the North-West, in Chile in the South. In
Chile, however, you also notice the presence of people of
mixed Indian and European blood in the rural population of
the Central Valley, and this even on the outskirts of Santiago. These Chilean mestizos are, of course, culturally
assimilated to the Chileans of wholly European blood, and
one sees no evidence, in Chile, of social discrimination on
racial lines.

Chile's geography is surprising. There are about 2,500
miles of coastline; and the Chilean navy has distinguished

itself, not only in the war of independence, but also in the war of 1879 against Peru and Bolivia. Yet the habitable part of the mainland of Chile is an almost entirely land-locked country. Though you can see across almost the whole breadth of even the broadest part of Chile in clear weather, the interior is cut off from the sea by a continuous coastal range through which the rivers that descend from the Andes force their way with difficulty. There are places, such as Valdivia, where a number of rivers, converging from several quarters of the compass, have had to join forces in order to break through the mountain barrier. The city of Valdivia stands at one such meeting-point of many waters. Travel by water from Valdivia to Corrál, Valdivia's port for ocean-going ships within sight of the open sea, and you will realize that only the united strength of a number of rivers could have compelled the coastal mountains to yield a passage. It is characteristic of Chile that its capital, Santiago, is sited, not on the coast, but in the Central Valley, at the western foot of the Andes. It is also characteristic that the great south road, running from Santiago to Puerto Montt, does not touch the coast at any point, though this road must be about 625 miles long. Its nearest point to the coast is at Valdivia, and Valdivia, like Santiago, is an inland city.

If you pivoted Chile round, through an angle of 180 degrees, and then transplanted it to the western end of the Old World, its tropical northern end would lie in the Sahara and its arctic southern end in the North Sea. In their configuration, Southern Chile and Northern Norway resemble each other. In these sections of the two countries, the mountains descend so precipitously to the sea that the communication between points on this coastline has to be by sea or by air. To carry roads or railways round or across the innumerable fjords would be a herculean task. In the southern third of Chile, south of Puerto Montt, the Central

Valley is submerged, and the coastal range is prolonged in the form of a chain of islands. Only the island of Chiloé, which is the northernmost of them and the biggest, preserves the configuration of Central Chile in miniature.

From the Sahara to the North Sea! Northern Chile is a desert; the northern half of Central Chile, round Santiago, is like some inland plain in the Mediterranean basin; the southern half of Central Chile is like Northern Europe. (This part of the country has been opened up by German settlers who are first-rate farmers in the North European style.) As you fly from Santiago to Puerto Montt, you can watch the rivers changing their character. Round Santiago they are seasonal torrents wandering over broad shingle-beds. Before you land at Puerto Montt, they have become smooth-flowing perennial streams.

From the Sahara to the North Sea! You might expect to meet, in Chile, every gradation of Eurafrican climatic zones. But, in climate, Chile is no Old-World country. From end to end, Chile is gripped between two refrigerators, the Andes to the east and the Humboldt current to the west. So, latitude for latitude, each section of Chile is decidedly colder than its European counterpart. I am writing these lines at Pucón, at the eastern end of Lake Villarica; and Pucón's latitude, translated into European terms, is equivalent to Lisbon's. Yet today, 23 October 1966, which corresponds to the Northern Hemisphere's 23 April, I am feeling as cold as I should be in early spring in North-West England—and North-West England is a chilly country at all seasons of the year.

Pucón

WHEN we skimmed over Lake Villarica and sighted the airstrip in the valley that runs up eastward from the head of the lake, our spirits were low. Our objective that morning had not been Pucón; it had been Chiloé Island. Before taking off from Valdivia we had ascertained that the weather over Chiloé was fair. This had been welcome news; for practicable flying weather over Chiloé is an uncommon boon. Our disappointment had therefore been the sharper when, as we were heading expectantly southward, our pilot re-checked the Chiloé weather news by radio and was told that the weather over Chiloé had already changed for the worse, and that we must turn about and make, instead, for some landing-place to the northward. Sure enough, before we had had time to reach the Lake of Villarica, our little plane had been buffeted and drenched by the bad weather that had ruled out our projected trip to the south. Our pilot had had to fight his way through wind and rain. Now we were east of Villarica Lake and were over the Pucón airstrip. But what was our pilot doing? Ignoring the airstrip, he flew on up the valley and then circled low, twice over. After that, he flew back over the airstrip, ignoring it once more, and made a similar double circle over a building on the edge of a wooded cliff overhanging the lake.

Could the pilot have lost his nerve? Was it possible that he was flinching from making a landing on that airstrip in the storm? No, surely this was inconceivable, for he was a pilot of high repute, and he had demonstrated his skill to us in riding the storm that morning. Our momentary misgiving was laid to rest when, at his third approach to the airstrip, he landed on it with ease. It then flashed across my mind that those two double circles had been, not symptoms of distress, but signals to friends on terra firma. Students of bees tell us that bees communicate with each other by performing a circular dance. Perhaps our pilot had been talking bee-language when he was making those double gyrations—and it now turned out that this was in fact what he had been doing. Up in the valley, he had been talking bee-wise to his sister and brother-in-law, who had a farm up there. Over the edge of the lake he had been talking bee-wise to the proprietor of the Antumalal Hotel, and, over each of these two points, he had gone on circling till he had obtained an answer by gesture. As we stepped out of the plane, the pilot's sister and brother-in-law arrived at the airstrip in one car and the hotelier's son in another.

We were now quickly reconciled to the temporary mis-carriage of our plans; for we found ourselves in a beautiful place as the guests of congenial hosts. All our hosts were Chileans, but only the pilot's sister was a Chilean of Spanish descent. Her husband was third-generation English; the creator and proprietor of the hotel and his wife were first-generation Czechs. The Anglo-Chilean farmer's grandfather had emigrated to this region of Chile to fell timber. The Czech family had come as refugees. When disaster had overwhelmed Czechoslovakia in 1938, the proprietor of the Antumalal Hotel had been a member of the Czech diplo-matic mission in Paraguay. Hitler had then given an un-foreseen turn to the young Czech diplomatist's career, and he had shown his mettle by responding triumphantly to the challenge.

From the Pucón airstrip next day, we succeeded, at the

second attempt, in flying almost as far as the south-eastern corner of Chiloé Island and in returning to Puerto Montt up the rugged coast of the South Chilean mainland. Our pilot here picked up a co-pilot and brought us back in a larger plane to the Pucón airstrip via Lake Todos los Santos (All Saints). He demonstrated his virtuosity by hoisting us over the shoulder of a high volcano. What next? A day and night of rest at Pucón before returning to work at Santiago? No, the weather decided against that. Next morning the clouds began to descend on the Pucón airstrip, and our two pilots decided that we must make a get-away after lunch. But, when we reached the airstrip, they found that we were already too late. Visibility was now too poor for risking a take-off. The alternative was a twelve-and-a-half-hour night-journey by train from Temúco to Santiago if I was to be in Santiago in time for my lecture there the next evening. We had reconciled ourselves to this fate, and had gone to bed in order to rest while we could, when there was a sudden urgent knock on our bedroom door. It was the pilots. If we drove to the airstrip at once, they reported, the cloud had now lifted just enough to make the take-off possible. For this there must be thirty metres of visibility from ground-level upwards, and, at the moment, there was just that.

We soared into the cloud, rose above it, broke our journey at Chillán in brilliant sunshine, to refuel and to eat a sandwich, landed by moonlight at Quintero airport, and slept that night at Viña del Mar, on the shore of the Pacific, next door to Valparaiso. We fell asleep, assured that, whatever the weather next morning, we should reach Santiago by road in time for me to keep my engagement there.

Two Chilean Harbours

CHILE'S coastline is about 2,500 miles long, but good harbours are rare there, and good harbours with easy access to productive hinterlands are rarer still. I have visited two of these exceptionally favoured Chilean ports, Valparaiso and Coquimbo. Valparaiso's hinterland is the Central Valley of Chile, which contains the country's massive capital city, Santiago. Coquimbo's hinterland is modest by comparison, but Nature has compensated Coquimbo by giving her two splendid natural harbours, and, though Coquimbo has not, in its hinterland, any counterpart of Santiago to sustain it, it does at least have La Serena—an educational centre in which 18,000 out of its 60,000 inhabitants are students of various ages. Moreover, Coquimbo's hinterland, like Valparaiso's, leads up eastwards to an important pass over the Andes. Coquimbo is the nearest seaport to the Argentinian oasis of San Juan; Valparaiso is the nearest to the much larger and more important Argentinian oasis of Mendoza. It goes without saying that the two port-cities that enjoy these natural advantages are old Spanish settlements. Coquimbo is old enough to have been sacked by Sir Francis Drake.

English pirates, from Drake onwards, made themselves a nuisance to successive Spanish captains-general of Chile; the more southerly of Coquimbo's two natural harbours became a favourite resort for buccaneers; but the English were welcomed eventually when, after Chile had achieved her independence, they came, this time, for the peaceful purpose of mining and smelting the local copper-ore. The size of the nineteenth-century English community at Coquimbo can be gauged by the number of burials in the English cemetery there. English? I have slipped into what, I fear, may be characteristic English arrogance in writing 'English' when a majority of the names on the tombstones are Welsh and Cornish. Of course they are Welsh and Cornish, considering that their bearers' business at Coquimbo was mining. Today there is only one representative of the United Kingdom in Coquimbo and La Serena together. She, too, is Cornish, but she is not a mining engineer; she is a teacher in a school. As for the rest of the once numerous British colony, they have melted away. Some families seem to have just died out; others have had the happier fortune of making money at Coquimbo and having then become members of the Chilean 'Establishment' in Santiago.

The copper-mines in the hinterland of Coquimbo have now been worked out. The productive Chilean copper-mines today lie farther to the north, with one big mine in the foothills of the Andes a short way to the south of Santiago. The nineteenth-century British copper-smelting works at the buccaneers' cove are now in ruins; and Coquimbo now lives principally on the export of unprocessed iron-ore to supply the Bethlehem steel-works in Pennsylvania. On the Orinoco River in Venezuela, I have seen ships of the same build loading with iron-ore from the two mountains made of iron about eight miles away from the river's southern bank. In the immediate neighbourhood there are waterfalls that can produce a virtually unlimited amount of hydro-electric power; and the Venezuelan Government has set up a steel-mill on the spot, to process Venezuelan ore with Venezuelan power on Venezuelan ground. There are no waterfalls at Coquimbo; the water that flows down the irrigation-channels from far up the valley is far too weak a trickle to do the job. Yet cannot Coquimbo find some source of power to process her iron-ore on the spot, as her copper-ore was once processed on the spot by British entrepreneurs? The talk of integrating Latin America economically—talk that is so much in the air in so many Latin American countries today —will remain ineffective unless and until Latin America develops enough industry, in the style of São Paulo, to absorb at least an appreciable portion of her immense output of primary products. Till that day arrives, each Latin American country is bound to continue to have closer economic intercourse with the industrial countries of Europe and North America than with its geographical neighbours in the New World to the south of the Rio Grande.

If and when that day does arrive, Latin America's once busy seaports will stagnate, as Recífe is already stagnating now that São Paulo is capturing from Europe and North America the business of supplying North-Eastern Brazil with consumer-goods. The Chilean ports that are exporting Chile's copper today will decay in their turn if and when Chile develops her industries to a point at which she consumes her copper herself and, at the same time, meets her demand for consumer-goods by creating a Chilean equivalent of São Paulo. To an amateur observer, it looks as if that day were still far off, and, in this connexion, a visit to the docks at Valparaiso is instructive. Valparaiso is not a copper-exporting port. The Chilean produce that we saw being loaded there on to a Norwegian ship was wool. In the Valparaiso docks, it looked as if the goods flowing in far exceeded in value the goods trickling out. The incoming commodities that we saw there ranged from Ecuadorian bananas to German machinery. This impression was superficial and might be misleading, yet it is borne out by the strain under which the Chilean currency's exchange value is labouring.

G

Evidently Valparaiso has seen its best days. Once it was Chile's principal business centre; by now, much of the business has migrated to the insatiable city of Santiago. All the same, Valparaiso is the most interesting of all Chilean cities for a European visitor. In its physical lay-out it is a South American counterpart of Genoa. The docks hug the foot of a steep mountain-side covered with streets and houses. Here, as in other Latin American cities, shanty-towns jostle with opulent middle-class quarters. At Valparaiso, though, and on the outskirts of Santiago too, there is an impressive amount of new municipal housing; and at Valparaiso the decent districts and the slums are serviced impartially by what looks like an adequate supply of public transport. Whatever Valparaiso's future may be, the city, in its present shape, breathes a spirit that commands even a casual visitor's respect.

The Present-day World in Venezuela

THERE are mirrors with a curvature that accentuates the features of the countenances that they reflect, and, in accentuating them, makes them unmistakably clear. Present-day Venezuela serves as a mirror of this kind. Visit Venezuela, and you will see, reflected there, the visage of the present-day world, with its characteristic features thrown into sharp relief.

Until after the beginning of the present century, Venezuela was not particularly prominent among the Latin American republics. It had, however, played a leading part in the liberation of the Spanish Empire of the Indies from Spanish rule. Indeed, it shared with Argentina the distinction of taking the initiative in liberating the rest of the vast Spanish dominions in the Americas. The Liberator Bolívar, who has given his name to far-away Bolivia, was a Venezuelan landowner. Venezuela and Argentina played this leading role in the early nineteenth-century war of liberation thanks to their geographical position. The Spanish colonial administration had tried to insulate the Spanish overseas empire from contact with the non-Spanish countries of the Western World. It had sought to prevent the entry of non-Spanish traders, and, still more, the arrival of the dangerous liberal ideas that non-Spanish visitors might bring with them. Venezuela and Argentina were the two provinces of the Spanish Empire in which this Spanish policy of insulation had been the least successful. Venezuela had, at her doors, the Dutch, French, and British West Indies; and, via the islands, eighteenth-century liberal thought had seeped into this adjoining part of the Spanish mainland. This piece of history has a bearing on current events. The biggest of the West Indies is Cuba. You fly over Cuba en route from Carácas, the capital of Venezuela, to Miami, the nearest big city in the United States. So it is conceivable that history might repeat itself by making Venezuela serve, for a second time, as the door for the penetration of revolutionary ideas into continental Latin America.

Until after the beginning of the present century, Venezuela was obscure because she was poor. She had been an importer of modern ideas, but had had little to export in exchange for these. Neither the Spanish imperial government nor the Spanish colonists nor the native Indian population had been aware of the natural wealth below their feet. They had thought of wealth in terms of gold and silver, and, for these minerals, Venezuela was of no account compared with Mexico and Peru. The story of Latin America's wealth has been like the story of the Arab World's wealth. The statesmen blithely drew international frontiers, at a venture, across vast unexplored territories. They were carefree in their allocation of territory that they believed to be of no appreciable value. It was not till after they had finished their haphazard work that Nature's equally haphazard distribution of her subterranean and subaqueous wealth came to light; and these natural accidents, in combination with the man-made vagaries of the international frontiers, made some countries fabulously rich, while leaving neighbour countries miserably poor.

Venezuela has been one of the lucky countries—lucky, that is, if one takes the conventional view that it is a blessing, not a curse, to become rich suddenly by chance. A few years before the outbreak of the First World War, prospectors discovered the oil-field round the edges, and under the surface, of Lake Maracaibo; and, some years after the end of the Second World War, other prospectors discovered mountains made of iron-ore, with a 65-per cent. metallic content, on the south side of the River Orinoco, below Angostura, where the new industrial city of Santo Tomé de Guayana is now arising. There is an irony about the fate of greedy people who tread on potential wealth without suspecting its presence underfoot. The city of Maracaibo, commanding the entrance to the huge lake that bears its name, and the city of Angostura, at the head of oceanic navigation up the course of the River Orinoco, were early Spanish foundations and almost as early objectives of English piratical enterprise. Drake sacked Maracaibo; Sir Walter Raleigh failed to take and sack Angostura in his desperate search for El Dorado. What could Drake have made of Lake Maracaibo's mineral oil if the god Poseidon, with a trident stroke, had made a gusher spout up from the lake like the blowing of a whale? And what would Raleigh have said if he had been told that the metallic wealth of the country that he was unsuccessfully invading consisted, not of romantic gold, but of prosaic iron? It was left to our own century to discover these stupendous Venezuelan mineral treasures and to exploit them.

As you fly, today, over the iron-mountains of Venezuelan Guayana, you see, below your wings, two huge lumps of rusty-red ore rising out of the plain. The bigger of the two— and it is by far the bigger—is still untouched. It is being held in reserve. The smaller iron-mountain would be a big one on any other standard than the size of its neighbour. This smaller mountain is now being gradually scraped away (underground mining is unnecessary), and the ore is being taken by train to the newly-built steel-mills in the angle above the junction of the Orinoco with its great southern

tributary the Caroní. Just before joining the Orinoco, the
Caroní tumbles over a ledge in a long line of falls. The
harnessing of one section of these has provided the infant
steel-mills with all the hydro-electric power that they need
so far. The potential supply is virtually unlimited. The
Caroní's tributary the Corrao has falls as fine as the Caroní's
own (they are unharnessed, up to date). And the Corrao is fed
by the Angel Falls, which are said to be the highest in the
World. (Our plane circled in front of them to give us a view.)
Then, next door to the iron, there is manganese. The only
thing locally lacking, for the present, is suitable coking
coal. The Guayana steel-mills import their coke from
England. Ocean-going ships load and unload at the steel-
mills' river port on the Orinoco. It is fortunate for England
that she has something to sell to Venezuela which Venezuela needs but cannot produce at home. This good fortune,
however, is unlikely to be very long-lasting.

As for the Lake Maracaibo oil-fields at the opposite
corner of Venezuela, you might imagine, as your plane
descends, that you were hovering over a vast armada of
sixteenth-century caravels and galeases. The caravels are
oil-well derricks; the galeases are weird-looking contraptions
for capturing natural gas from below the lake bottom. For
twenty or thirty miles out into the lake from its eastern
shore, its surface is studded with extraordinary bits of
elaborate apparatus. It is an astonishing spectacle.

Being now a treasure-house, Venezuela has become a land
of contrasts and inequalities and consequently a land of
unrest. In present-day Venezuela, as in the present-day
World as a whole, one is conscious of a tension in the air.
Was the atmosphere as tense, I wonder, in the days—still
not so long ago—when poverty was the Venezuelan people's
common lot, and when even the largest Venezuelan landowners were no millionaires? The housing of the Venezuelan

workers of the lowest category in the Shell Company's camp at Lagunillas presents a harrowing contrast to the squalor of the fishing village of Pueblo Viejo, which stands embedded in the oil-field like a festering fly in amber. Even here, life has improved. The villagers no longer drink the lake water beneath their pile dwellings. The Shell Company has piped pure water to them from its own supply. All the same, the contrast is sharp; and it is even sharper in Carácas, where shacks jostle with tall buildings made of glass and concrete in an ultra-modern style of architecture, while super-throughways cut across primitive mule-tracks.

The shacks are pathetic monuments to unfulfilled expectations. Since a golden rain from the oil-fields and the iron-mountains began to descend on the capital, the poverty-stricken subsistence-farming peasantry has been streaming out of the countryside into the city in the hope that some of the wealth-giving drops may fall into their mouths. Perhaps one in a thousand finds this dream come true. Meanwhile, the rest of the migrants are now living in urban slum conditions that are still worse than their ancestral lot. They would have fared less badly if they had stayed at home and had continued to wring a bare subsistence out of the flanks of the Andes. But what peasant, anywhere in the World, is willing today to be convinced that a migration from the country to the city is not going to bestow on him all the fabled amenities of urban life? The shanty-towns of Carácas are duplicated in those of Arequipa and Calcutta and Baghdad.

Here is a polarization of extremes of wealth and poverty. Polarization creates high tension, and high tension generates destructive sparks. Today Venezuela is afflicted with sabotage and terrorism. But there is a paradox here again. This violence is what one would expect, yet it does not proceed from the expected quarter. It does not come from the

urban shanty-towns or from the rural slums out of which
these have been populated. It comes from the university
campuses. Yet the university students are not members of
the 'have-not' majority of the Venezuelan people. Quite a
generous shower of the golden rain has come the students'
way. In the national university at Carácas there are no
tuition fees. Venezuela can afford this, but she can hardly
afford the students' reaction. No doubt it is only a fraction
of the student-body that reacts to prosperity in the violent
way; but this fraction is enough to keep Venezuela in a
fever. Here we have the present-day state of the World
accentuated with a vengeance.

The iron-mountains of the Orinoco basin are being
converted into ingots of steel by the Venezuelan Government's own enterprise. The oil industry is largely in the
hands of foreign companies. Shell is a joint Dutch and
British enterprise; Creole is North American. For capitalistic
enterprise, Venezuela is a bed of thorns, and it is naturally
even thornier for foreign capital than it is for Venezuelan.
The foreign companies that are operating in Venezuela are
following an enlightened policy. They are wisely trying to
make their presence agreeable to the Venezuelan people by
performing for it a number of services that are of unquestionable value for Venezuela's national development. On the
companies' staffs, more and more Venezuelans are being
employed in more and more responsible positions. The
companies are, in fact, making themselves serve as schools
in which Venezuelans can learn to master the latest arts of
modern technology. The companies are also doing dis-
interested work for Venezuela in fields that are quite
unconnected with their own commercial operations. Shell,
for instance, maintains an experimental agricultural station
at Cagua with a budget of about one million pounds
sterling a year. In the first ten years of its existence, this

philanthropic enterprise has already done much to help Venezuelan farmers to raise the standard of their production.

Venezuela has the makings of an earthly paradise. It would, in fact, be one if a paradise could be stocked solely with minerals and plants, without needing any complement of human inhabitants. Human nature is the crux. Venezuelan human nature is probably no better and no worse than the general run of the mill. Venezuelan wealth, however, is something quite out of the ordinary, and extraordinary wealth puts human nature to one of its hardest tests. Can human nature stand this? That is the critical question today for Venezuela, as it is for the World as a whole. And the outcome in Venezuela, whatever it may be, is bound to be of world-shaking importance. If, in Venezuela, the spirit of President Kennedy's Alliance for Progress were to suffer defeat, that would be the opportunity for President Castro. Present-day Venezuela is as great a prize as a sixteenth-century Spanish treasure-galleon. Into whose hands is this prize going to fall?

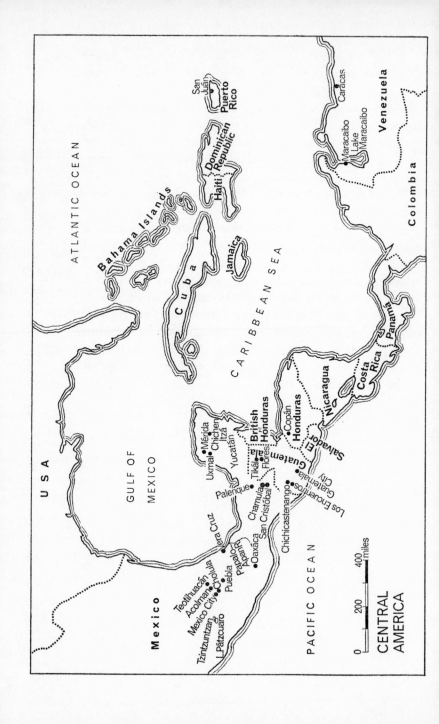

CENTRAL
AMERICA

Tikál

Suddenly the glittering surface of the Caribbean gave way to a low grey coast, and I knew where I was. We were gliding down over henequen plantations towards the airport of Mérida in Yucatán, and for an instant, before we took off again, I spied the two great towers of the city's cathedral on the skyline. Now we were flying over the bush. Who would guess, from the air, that this fresh green coverage of saplings, and the limestone shelf from which it springs, are bone-dry? I could see through that deceptive dewy look, for I had walked about, down below there, five years ago. But now we are heading for new ground. We are bound for the rain-forest of Northern Guatemala, which has submerged the ruins of the temples and palaces of the Maya civilization in its Classic Age. What shall I manage to see en route from Mérida to Guatemala City? As I peer out of the window, I cannot register any dramatic change in the landscape; yet, after an hour's flight, it has changed indeed. Now I am looking down on what I have seen from the air over the Amazon Basin and over Eastern Sumatra: a close-knit stand of huge trees of many shapes and shades. Here too they crowd so close together that there is no room for a dead tree to fall. No road thrusts its way through them; nothing parts them but water: an occasional lakelet and then the writhing coils of the Pasión River. No pinnacles of Maya masonry emerge above the tree-tops. Yet we must be passing over dozens of famous Maya sites. And now the jungle ends as abruptly as the Caribbean. The flat forest turns into a choppy sea of shorn hills which seem to spring up at our plane as she skims over them. These hills are full of life. They have fields on their flanks and cottages on their summits and footpaths winding along their ridges. These approaches to Guatemala City are, once again, a living human world. But where are the dead cities of the Maya?

Well, now we are retracing our flight in a smaller plane at a lower altitude. The human highlands have died down into the inhospitable forest; and this time, as we stall and dip and wheel to make the Tikál airstrip, three great pinnacles do flash past above the tree-tops. A few days later I am gazing at all three of them—and at Temple Five and the huge South Acropolis as well—from a vantage-point just below the towering roof-comb of Temple Four. Tikál is the largest and most imposing of all Classic Maya ceremonial centres—the most imposing but not the most beautiful, for both Palenque and Copán, in their different ways, surpass Tikál in beauty of setting and beauty of detail. But at Tikál there are no less than six temples of cathedral height and volcano contours. The higher they soar, the nearer their battered build approaches the perpendicular. They were bent upon exceeding the highest height to which the tallest tree could grow; for they knew from the start that they could not count on their human servitors' aid for keeping the trees at bay till the end of time. Sooner or later, Man would fade out of the picture again; and then these piles of man-hewn stones would be left to fight it out with the vengeful forest. So at birth, while they can still command lavish human labour, these temples must make sure of soaring so high that no tree can ever rob them of their access to the Sun.

When, at Tikál, one stands in the central plaza, Temples One and Two close the ends, and piles of masonry encase either side—vertical temples along one side and horizontal palaces along the other. Here one has the illusion of being able to take in the whole lay-out at a single glance. The extent of Tikál slowly dawns on one as one stumbles upon terrace behind terrace and acropolis behind acropolis. One of the first steps taken by the archaeologists of the present University of Pennsylvania mission was to cut rides through the forest from the airstrip to the principal monuments. Between one group of temples and another one may walk for thirty or forty minutes along one of these newly-cut paths; and the initiated guide will point out, through the trees on either hand, the distant parapets of the broad ancient causeway along which the new path is threading its way. When the paths give out, a man armed with a compass and a machete slashes a track for the visitor through the undergrowth, and one is almost incredulous when he casually remarks that, four or five inches below this savage surface, the original pavement of a smothered plaza is still intact. You can't believe it? Well, look where this tree has fallen, or where this animal has dug its burrow. The upturned fragments of the buried pavement are scattered round the hole. The plaster speaks, and there can be no doubt about its veracity. All these square leagues of wilderness were once Man's submissive domain. Yet now Nature reigns again, as she reigned before Man first set to work, with flint and obsidian blades, to fell the trees and square the stones and banish Nature to the horizon.

Today, we human beings walk here on sufferance. One morning, at the foot of the South Acropolis, we walked into a column of army ants. In an instant they were swarming over our legs and half way up our bodies. No matter how many we might kill, millions more were marching on. They were invincible because they were expendable, and the only salvation lay in flight—though this meant scaling the Southern Acropolis's almost perpendicular side.

Why on earth did the Maya plant their principal ceremonial centre at Tikál of all places? The huge reservoirs there are as staggering as the lofty pinnacles. But why choose a site which required the building of such mighty works to catch and hold the annual rains, when, a few miles away, there are the spring-fed waters of Lake Petén and, a few miles beyond that, the rolling stream of the River Pasión flowing into the River Usumacinta? The Maya did not despise these potable and partly navigable waters. On the banks of the River Usumacinta they founded the centres now know as Altar de Sacrificios and Bonampák and Piedras Negras, and in the opposite quarter, south-eastward, Copán stands beside a running river. Yet Tikál and its sister Uaxactún were deliberately sited in a landscape without rivers or springs—on limestone through which you do not strike water, however deep you sink your well.

Why were these mighty buildings raised? Were they solitary sanctuaries or the nuclei of populous cities? Were they surrounded by continuous stretches of built-up and cultivated areas? Or were the fields, then as now, temporary glades burnt out of the forest to be abandoned again, for another eight or ten years, after one or two harvests had been snatched from them? If the peasants raised their crops by the same primitive methods as their present descendants, how were they persuaded or compelled to spend their hard-won surplus of food and leisure on building these vast piles and maintaining the astronomer-priests who made use of them? And what were the circumstances in which these ceremonial centres were eventually abandoned? Did agriculture begin to bring in diminishing returns, while the priests increased their exactions from the peasantry in the hope of appeasing the wrath of the gods? Did the peasants lose faith in their religious mentors? And, if so, did they cut their throats or just leave them to starve? There were certainly crises in which, if throats were not cut, calendrical stelae were deliberately defaced. But that is all that the mutilated monuments can tell us. In the end, Tikál and its sisters were left to the mercy of the forest; and the writhing roots have been clutching the shapely stones and prising them asunder for more than a thousand years, till our present-day archaeologists intervened in the battle on the hard-pressed masonry's side. We can save these monuments, but can we read their secret? This is the question that makes Middle American archaeology so fascinating a quest.

Flores

THREE days ago, en route to Tikál, we had touched down on this airstrip along the south shore of Lake Petén and had looked longingly across the water to the city of Flores, perched on its dome-shaped island. Today we are back again, and this time with an hour to spare. So we charter a dug-out punt with an outboard motor and chug through reeds and cormorants to the landing-place below the billiard-room which is now the city's social centre.

No wheel has ever rolled into Flores; no quadruped has ever trodden its streets. Till the advent of the aeroplane the only means of access from the outer world was to hack one's way with a machete through hundreds of miles of jungle. Yet Flores is, in miniature, a complete Spanish city—which is as much as to say a Roman city laid out according to the age-old specifications given in the handbooks of the Roman surveyors. Though the streets are grass-grown for lack of wheels and hooves, they are broad and cobbled, with side-walks to shelter the pedestrian from an imaginary vehicular traffic. On the crown of the hill there are a miniature plaza, miniature cathedral, and miniature governor's palace. And in the principal street there is at least one store so well-stocked that, in a country town in the United States, it would have claimed to be a super-market. All the canned goods on its shelves must have been flown in by air at a price, yet there are plenty of buyers. For, after all, Flores is one of those lucky cities in which money has to be spent.

photo Paul Popper, London

V Argentina: Salta, a glen

photo by Nick de Morgoli, Camera Press, London

VI Venezuela: Carácas

Flores is the capital of the Petén—the jungle half of Guatemala—and the Petén is the source of the chicle which provides the United States with its chewing-gum. From Flores the chicleros range the jungle; you cannot walk ten yards into it without seeing the gashes that their machetes have made on the sap-laden tree-trunks. They know the jungle from end to end, including not only the richest stands of chicle-bearing trees and the choicest stands of mahogany and other rare timbers, but a score of smothered Maya sites that have not yet found their way on to the charts of the eager archaeologists. The chiclero is a match for the forest that has eventually got the better of the Maya astronomer-priest. He can find his way; he can fend off the jaguars that prowl by night; and, if his rations of water give out a hundred miles away from the nearest spring or river, he knows of a vine that stores water for him and keeps it sweet. So the chiclero lives to make periodic visits to the capital of his jungle-empire, and he spends the money that he is paid for his jungle-spoil as freely as the cowboy used to spend his, eighty years ago, in western towns in the United States. Therefore Flores is prosperous, and it is choosy. For instance, it chooses to live on air-borne maize-flour and black beans—leaving to the cormorants the excellent fish with which Lake Petén swarms. In Flores there are consequently more cormorants than human beings.

Life is changing in Flores today. On the mainland, west of the airstrip, there now stands a fine large school. It is linked with the island by a long plank gangway on stilts, and it dwarfs the municipal buildings on the crown of the hill. But the lake and the island have seen greater changes in the past. Look at that jungle-covered peninsula that juts westward into the lake and overtops the island-city. Those smothered mounds were once Maya temples—perhaps of the Classic Age—and their pinnacles must once have soared high

H

above the level of the present Spanish cathedral's belfry. Nor was this the only chapter of Maya history by the waters of Lake Petén; for Spanish-Roman Flores is believed to stand on the site of a Maya settlement that preserved its political independence and lived its traditional life down to the closing years of the seventeenth century.

When the Spanish conquest struck Middle America and Peru in the sixteenth century with the force of a tornado and laid empires and civilizations flat, a few survivors of the catastrophe managed to find temporary shelter beyond the immediate reach of the conqueror's long arm. In Peru an Inca-led resistance-movement held out for a generation in the montaña, the jungle-clad Atlantic slope of the Andes. In Mayaland, when the Spaniards swooped upon the comparatively open bush of dry Yucatán, one Maya people, the Itzá, trekked southward—below the present air-trail from Mérida to Guatemala City—and found a new home on the shore of Lake Petén—probably on Flores Island itself. Here they lived on, unharassed by the Spaniards and, for most of the time, actually unknown to them, for more than 150 years, till Spanish missionary enterprise eventually brought them to light and consequently into danger. The missionaries and the Spanish Crown would probably have been content with a nominal conversion to Christianity and recognition of Spanish sovereignty, and it looked as if a peaceful agreement were in sight when a Spanish military expedition made its adventurous way to Lake Petén through the jungle from Mérida. Unhappily, fighting broke out after all, and the last of the Itzá were destroyed instead of being peacefully and gradually assimilated. It is not even certain that their secluded city stood where Flores stands today.

All that remains of them is the memory of a horse which is said to have been left in their hands by a wandering Spanish conquistador of the first generation. Believing this unearthly being to be a god, the Itzá honoured it by feeding it first on flowers and then on meat, and they were desolated when it died of this god-like diet. Right down to the Spanish conquest of their city of refuge in the sixteen-nineties, they religiously preserved the horse's skeleton, or perhaps a stone image of it. In the final catastrophe this is said to have been thrown into the lake, and the Spanish inhabitants of Flores assert that, when the water is clear, the skeleton or statue can still be seen lying on the lake-bottom. This tall story is all that remains of the last stronghold of the pre-Columbian civilization of the Maya.

Copán

It is now 10 a.m. and we are still on the ground, though we were booked to take off at seven and had therefore risen at dawn. Shall we make it? This is the only day we have for visiting Copán; and Copán ranks with Palenque and Tikál as one of the three most illuminating monuments of the Maya civilization in its Classic Age. Long ago the airport—we are in Guatemala City—has come alive. Huge intercontinental planes are busily coming in and taking off, and a U.S. Army helicopter is making a round of practice flights. How many times, by now, I wonder, has this tiresome machine trailed its feet on the runway below the windows of the control-tower café and then taken off with a roar to repeat the same monotonous performance a few minutes later? How much more useful to us, and also more instructive for the crew, if it were to occur to them that they might spend their time and fuel on conveying us to Copán. Our intended conveyance is a single-engine Cessna plane; but the control-tower's regulations for Cessnas are severe. A higher standard of visibility is required for them than for other aircraft before they are allowed to take to the air, and the visibility is still below standard today at 10 a.m. In fact, to our amateur eyes it looks as if it were getting worse instead of better, for we have chosen an unfortunate date for our venture. In Middle America, April is the last month of the dry season, and this is the month in which the peasants are burning off the forest to make their *milpas*, temporary fields fertilized by wood-ash. All around us, columns of smoke are pouring up to thicken the haze in the sky. But our pilot—son of a Cantabrian father and a Neapolitan mother—is as resourceful as he is reassuring. Just when we have mournfully given up hope he announces that he has allayed the control-tower's scruples and we are off.

We are off, indeed, into the grey; for the haze soon blots out the plateau on which Guatemala City stands. But a single-engined Cessna is no Viscount. It cannot part company with the earth and navigate outer space; and, since it cannot climb above the mountains, it must dodge between them. So we do dodge, with a furry volcano-top looming up at us out of the haze on this side and a higher mountain-flank on that side, and those innumerable columns of smoke doing their worst to thicken the murk. If our pilot did not inspire such confidence, I should begin to be frightened— and now, for a moment, I really am, for what is this coastline that is suddenly opening up ahead of us? What can it be but the coast of the Atlantic? And, if it is, then our pilot must have lost his way and overshot his mark. As we sail out over the sea, I hold my breath, till, to my relief, I spy a farther shore. After all this is not the Atlantic; it is a mountain-girt lake where the frontiers of Guatemala, Salvador, and Honduras meet; and we are bound for Honduras. So, after all, our pilot knows what he is about. He wheels and winds his way down a steeply descending valley, and at the end of this the airstrip of Rosa de Copán comes into view. Another snag: a largeish Honduran plane is lolling across the strip, about a third of the way along it, and shows no intention of getting out of our light. But our pilot is equal to the occasion. He manages to land us between the Honduran plane and the runway's end. A brief passport inspection, and we are off again—this time for Copán itself—and again we have a happy landing.

How shall I describe Copán? It is as distinctively Maya as its sisters Tikál and Palenque, yet it is surprisingly different in atmosphere from either of these. It does not overwhelm you, as Tikál does: its lines are horizontal, not vertical. Its workmanship has not the elegance of Palenque's, and it does not stand, as Palenque does, on the foot of a jungle-clad mountain with a view over a boundless plain. Copán lies in a smiling fertile valley, with rich deep volcanic soil, traversed by a river that sings as it ripples past. At Copán there is no jungle lying in wait to take its revenge on its human violators. Nature, in this happy valley, is asking to be tamed. The tension between Nature and Man is altogether lower here; so Man has enjoyed a margin for experimentation. There is a larger number of calendrical stelae at Copán than at all other known Classic Maya sites put together; and the sculptured human figure here is stepping out of the bas-relief and growing into the round. If Copán had continued to be a going concern for just a few generations longer, we may guess that it would have produced a three-dimensional statuary that could have rivalled that of India or Greece.

Why was Copán abandoned at the same date as her jungle-encircled sisters? At Copán the mystery of the collapse of the Classic Maya civilization reaches its climax; for the Copán River has never ceased to flow, and the volcanic soil of the valley has never refused to produce crops. No economic stress can have moved the peasant, here, to revolt against the priest or have moved the priest-king to despair of the republic. Yet the same impulse that led to the abandonment of Tikál and Palenque was operative at Copán too; and, for more than a thousand years past, there has been no life in this great ceremonial centre which the happy valley was so easily able to support. The mystery thickens, like the haze from the burning bush.

Chichicastenango

I N the highlands of Guatemala, civilization has not known
the vicissitudes through which it has passed on the jungle-
clad northern plains. In the highlands the pre-Classic Maya
civilization struck root at least as early as in the North; yet
in the Classic Age, when the cities on the plain burst into
flower, the highlands failed to distinguish themselves. The
strength of the Maya civilization in the highlands lies not in
brilliance but in staying-power; for in the highlands the
Maya people and their way of life are still a going concern,
whereas the Classic sites of the Maya civilization in the
Petén have relapsed into the wilderness.

On this afternoon of Easter Sunday, 1958, I am standing
on the top of a green hill—a furry tree-covered volcano—
which rises just outside the escarpment of the natural fastness
of Chichicastenango. On the summit sits the little shiny
black figure of a Maya god, and here is a Maya family
offering flowers and incense, on this Easter afternoon, to
their traditional pre-Christian object of worship. Just one
family is worshipping here; but in the city, on the steps of
St. Thomas's church, a crowd of worshippers is heaping
incense on a flaming altar, while others are lighting candles
whose smoke rises above the church's roof. Enter the nave,
and you will find a galaxy of candles and a host of
worshippers chanting prayers. What divinity are they
invoking? Christ or Tláloc, the Maya rain god? If you
questioned them it is probable that they would be unable to

draw the distinction; for, in their hearts and imaginations, the exotic religion imported by their Spanish conquerors has blended inextricably with their traditional practices and beliefs.

In the background the Catholic priest of St. Thomas's church hovers uneasily, like a hen whose supposed chickens have plunged, with ducklings' zest, into the waters. Is he to assert himself or to efface himself? Well, at any rate, he is better off than the priest who is nominally in charge of the church in the village of Chamula on the Las Casas plateau on the Mexican side of the border. At Chichicastenango the priest's presence in his church is tolerated by his Indian congregation, even at the high pagan festival of Easter Day, whereas at Chamula the priest dare not show his face more than once a year. In the Guatemalan highlands the Catholic Church has reaped her due reward for a policy that has been wise and generous. The Church has accepted the people's pre-Columbian religion as 'a preparation for the Gospel', and she prefers to see them celebrate their pagan rites within her walls and under her auspices. In the cloister of the dissolved monastery to which St. Thomas's church is attached, the missionary order by which the church is now served has installed a clinic and a school. The ascent from one religion to the other has been aligned through a course of health and knowledge. Will the Indians, sooner or later, rise to Christianity at, say, its Neapolitan level? Who can tell? But, meanwhile, who can be blind to the probability that, if pagan rites were banned within the church's precincts, St. Thomas's church would be empty on Easter Day, while the little black idol on the top of the neighbouring volcano would be receiving the homage of a throng of worshippers, and not just of one single ultra-conservative family?

It is evening, and the Indian families are preparing to return to their distant villages among the mountains. They are loading their mules with what they have bought—or have not managed to sell—at the Easter market in the plaza between the church of St. Thomas and the church of the Calvaria, which faces the larger church symmetrically. Some of the men (none of the women) are dropping in their tracks, dead drunk with fire-water distilled from sugar-cane. This, too, is part of the traditional celebration of the feast. Yet the general impression made by the Indians on the modern visitor is one of worth and strength. They hold steadfastly to their ancient ways while the rising tide of standardized modern civilization laps round them and seeps up the cañons almost to the level of the scarped plateaux on which their villages are perched.

We follow one party on its way out of town. The mule-track skirts the edge of a deep wooded gorge that bounds the fastness of Chichicastenango on one side. At first the track keeps on the level; then it suddenly dips down, and we can see it winding up the far-off opposite mountain-side. How many ups and downs, of that precipitousness, before the Easter pilgrims reach their home? We recoil from following them even on their first descent, and strike off at an angle along the Chichicastenango plateau's rim, only to lose our way and find it again just before sunset.

Have the Maya lost their way in a world in which modern science and technology are now paramount, or are they going to outlive the alien civilization that is threatening to engulf them? Perhaps my grandchildren may live to learn the answer to this enigmatic question.

Yucatán

I F the landscape is your prime concern in your tour in Latin America, and if you are pressed for time, make your way from Guatemala into Mexico through Chiapas, and leave Yucatán unvisited. In Yucatán the landscape is tame. Low bush does duty here for the soaring forest that envelops Tikál and threatens Palenque; and the mountains of Chiapas and Tabasco, on whose easternmost spur Palenque stands, are replaced in Yucatán by a series of limestone ridges that are so low that their undulations are hardly perceptible. At first sight, Yucatán gives the impression of being a relatively hospitable country. The bush looks traversable, and the freshness of its green suggests that the soil from which it springs must be moist. On closer acquaintance, however, this inviting impression proves to be an illusion. Green though the bush that covers Yucatán may be, the land is rocky and bone-dry. In Yucatán there are no rivers, streams, or springs. Water is to be found only in the *cenotes*. These are pot-holes, some of them of gigantic size, which have been created by a local collapse of the limestone crust that seals down the rest of the country. If, then, you are travelling in quest of beautiful or dramatic scenery, you can omit Yucatán from your itinerary without regret. If, however, your prime concern is with the history and the archaeology of pre-Columbian Middle America, then a visit to Yucatán is imperative for you. It is imperative because Yucatán's role in Middle American history is unique in at least two points.

In the first place, Yucatán is the only province of the Mayan World in which every phase of the Mayan culture, from beginning to end, is represented without any break.

To the south and south-west of Yucatán, from Copán through Tikál and Piedras Negras to Palenque, the sites that flourished in the Classical Age were suddenly abandoned, one after another. The cause of this abrupt ending of a high culture is unknown. There is no indication that the Classic Mayan culture was wrecked by barbarian invaders. A number of alternative hypotheses have been put forward. Perhaps the rain failed; perhaps the fertility of the soil round each of these sites was exhausted by over-cultivation; perhaps the peasants lost faith in the astronomer-priests' ability to compel the rain-god and the vegetation-god to perform their functions—a performance that had to be guaranteed if human life was to survive in this unpropitious environment. Perhaps the disillusioned and exasperated peasantry had eventually massacred the priests and had left the forest free to work its will on the temples and palaces that the peasants had built, at the priests' bidding, in faith that their hard labour would win for them, as the priests had declared that it would, the favour of the gods without which it was impossible for Man to live. Each of these hypotheses is supported by some of the experts; no hypothesis has won universal acceptance so far. The debate among the scholars continues, and the archaeological evidence may not ever suffice to give a conclusive answer to the enigmatic question. To an amateur's eye, the rows of identical glyphs of the rain-god suggest that the makers of them were in a desperate state of mind. On the faint chance that sheer reiteration might perhaps force the niggardly god's hand, it looks as if the makers of those glyphs had been prepared to reproduce the same prayer, carved in stone, any number of times over. Was this agonizing series of glyphs the handiwork of priests who were painfully aware that the peasants' belief in them was failing?

The cause of the abandonment of the Classic sites of the Mayan culture outside Yucatán is an open question, but it is a certain fact that, in Yucatán, the Mayan culture survived, in a succession of post-Classic phases, right down to the time of the Spanish conquest in the sixteenth century.

The second point in which the local history of the Mayan culture is unique is that, in Yucatán in the post-Classic Age, there was a fusion between the Mayan and the Mexican variety of the Middle American culture. In this age, Toltec warriors from the plateau seem to have established themselves in Yucatán either as conquerors of the local Maya or as mercenaries in their service. At any rate, the spirit of the plateau now imposed itself on the peninsula. It has been mentioned that the abandonment of the Classic sites of the Mayan culture, outside Yucatán, does not seem to have been caused by acts of war. In fact, the Mayan society of the Classic Age seems to have been singularly pacific. The only archaeological evidence for warfare in the Mayan World in this age is in the paintings discovered in the north-west, at Bonampák. Negative evidence is, of course, inconclusive. The Maya of the Classic Age may have been more violent and more bloodthirsty than they appear to have been on the evidence of their surviving monuments. If they were not addicted to war, they may have been addicted to human sacrifice. At any rate, in the post-Classic Mayan-Mexican culture of Yucatán, human sacrifice had evidently become a key institution and, in consequence, war had become a key institution too, since the victims for sacrifice were provided by prisoners captured in battle. The evidence of the monuments at Chichen Itzá suggests that, in this age, the lust for taking human life had become obsessive—indeed, maniacal. The revealing monuments are elegant but gruesome.

The warriors' ascendancy in Yucatán in this age was shared by the merchants. The priests, who had been dominant in the Classic Age, seem to have been permanently deposed. Their deposition may have been deserved; they may have become both exigent and ineffective; yet the sequel to the priests' régime makes the fall of this régime seem a misfortune in retrospect.

The priests were still reigning at the Classic sites to the south of Chichen Itzá, in the range of hills called the Puuc. Here, at Uxmal and Kabah, the sensitive visitor, who has recoiled from Chichen, can find beauty without horror. Sensitive? The warriors who slaughtered their human hecatombs at Chichen might challenge our claim to this epithet if they could come back to life and inspect our present-day world. They used to take human lives by the hundred with their obsidian blades. We take them by the hundred thousand with our bombs. Murder does not cease to be murder when it is committed at long range. Our modern technology has enabled us to commit murder on a scale that was far beyond the capacity of the most blood-thirsty pre-Columbian murderer in the age of the Middle American civilization's obscene decadence. The present-day visitor to Chichen should think twice before he lets fly. The missile in his hand may prove to be, not a sling-stone, but a boomerang.

Palenque

ON the night of 6 May, 1953, it was pouring at Villa Hermosa, and our spirits were as thoroughly dampened as the atmosphere. If it went on doing this much longer, the air-taxi that we had ordered for the next morning would not be able to take off, and then we should have either to abandon our projected visit to Palenque or else to shoot our time-table to pieces by waiting for the next train. (There was a train about twice a week.) Palenque was one of our prime objectives in Mexico, so our hearts were in our mouths, but happily our forebodings proved to have been too pessimistic. Our Cessna plane did take off, after all, according to plan. Skimming eastwards, between the mountains and the sea, over alternating swamp and scrub, the little creature soon began to descend towards a landing-strip on a rare patch of dry level ground; and, as we sank down, Palenque flashed past us on our right—a patch of white flaring out from the dark mass of the forest that clothes the mountains' eastern-most spurs as far as the point where the mountains give way to the valley of the Usumacinta River. A short drive from the landing-strip, first over low ground and then up a climbing road, and we found ourselves on the site.

Palenque, like Copán, is one of the grand monuments of the Mayan civilization in its Classic Age. The two sites lie at opposite extremities of the miniature Mayan World—Copán on Mayaland's south-eastern and Palenque on its north-western edge. The two sites are like each other in their splendour, but in their physical setting and in their spirit they are poles apart. Palenque is as splendidly sombre as Copán is splendidly joyous. Copán lies low on the bank of its river; Palenque stands high above the coastal swamp and scrub. It stands on a ledge on the mountain-side, with a wide view northward and eastward—a wide view now that the site has been extricated from the enveloping forest. To free this small patch of the works of Man from tropical Nature's grip had been a labour of Hercules; to keep it free was going to be more arduous still; for the tropical forest, like a tiger, holds Palenque between its paws. East and west and south, the forest shrouds the mountain-side. Palenque is forest-free only on sufferance.

We were visiting Palenque at an unusually dramatic moment even in the exciting history of the archaeologists' operations there. Till a few months before, it had been supposed, on the strength of the existing state of the evidence, that Middle American pyramids did not have the same function as their Egyptian counterparts. It had been supposed that, whatever the function of the Middle American pyramids might have been, they had not been built to serve as tombs. But now this assumption had been exploded by a thrilling discovery at Palenque. A slab on the summit of one of the pyramids there had proved to conceal a staircase, and this staircase had proved to lead down to a burial-chamber in which a Mayan prince was still lying in state with all his magnificent funeral gear intact. The finest of these treasures was the jade mask that had covered the dead man's face. (We saw this mask afterwards at Mérida, in the local director of archaeology's house there. The director was reassembling the scattered pieces of the jade mosaic before sending this gorgeous jigsaw puzzle to the National Museum in Mexico City.)

The pyramids and temples and stelae at Palenque have

been described and illustrated in more than one admirable study by an expert hand; so I will not give an amateur's rendering of these professional publications. I will take Man's works at Palenque for granted, and will concentrate on Nature's. These have not been so meticulously catalogued as Man's have been, and they are more difficult to illustrate than museum pieces are.

We spent only two nights in the archaeologists' quarters at Palenque, but those two nights have left on me some ineffaceable impressions—the nights more than the intervening day, and the darkness before dawn, as well as the shades of evening.

At nightfall the kindling of a light indoors gave the signal for an instant bombardment of the close-meshed wire-screen with which all the windows and doors of the building were fenced in. Insects of all shapes and sizes, from gigantic beetles downwards, now hurled themselves against the wire *en masse*. They struck the wire with such force that many of them fell dead or stunned. The screen was effective, yet the spectacle was terrifying. It made one aware of the ascendancy of the titanic insect world over our puny human world—the world exemplified in Man's ambitious works at Palenque. I had, of course, been aware of the biologists' estimates of the respective quantities of insect life and other life on this planet in terms of cubic feet. I had noted that the number of cubic feet of insect life far exceeded the combined total mustered by all the mammals, birds, reptiles, fishes, crustaceans, and plankton. But, till that first evening at Palenque, these figures had, for me, been nothing more than intellectual counters; they had made no impression on my imagination or on my feelings. Now the figures touched me to the quick.

At dawn we had a second reminder that Man is not the only tenant of this planet; and, this time, the experience

photo Paul Popper, London

VII Mexico: Palenque

VIII Mexico: Cholula

photo Paul Popper, London

was not eerie; it was enchanting. At dawn, a host of birds started to sing in a gamut of different calls. Each tune was sweet, and the singing went on, full-throated, from dawn till sunrise.

However, the most potent form of non-human life at Palenque was not the birds and not the insects; it was the vegetation. Its vitality was so strong that you could almost see the tendrils growing while you watched. On the road leading up to the site, rows on rows of tendrils had advanced from either side over the metalled surface till they had all but met. On the pyramids and temples and stelae, the work of disengaging these from the tendrils' embrace was soon going to have to be done all over again. But those shooting tendrils were just the forest's aggressive advance-guard. The advance-guard was startling; the forest itself was awe-inspiring. What is more, it was commanding and alluring.

This was my first encounter with the tropical forest; I had not met it yet, as I was to meet it later, in Guatemala and Peru and Sumatra and Cambodia; and a first acquaintance with the tropical forest is a unique experience. The tropical forest is not beautiful, as the temperate forest can be. Here there is never any tracery-pattern of light and shade, for the sunshine never penetrates this forest's close-matted roof. There are no autumn colours either; for, in the tropics, there are no seasons. The tropical forest is perennially moist and green. Moreover, at Palenque, at any rate, the forest does not even harbour any savage wild beasts. It is savage enough in itself to intimidate any human beings whom it may have enticed into its depths. When, during our first night at Palenque, the forest gave sound, the roarings were mighty enough to be the voice of lions and tigers, or, at the least, of pumas and jaguars. We pictured these crouching behind the massive tree-trunks, poised to spring upon their prey. We learned next day that what we had

I

been hearing was the voice of monkeys, groaning in unison to keep each other company in the dark. We never caught sight of them, for their home was on the upper surface of the forest's matted roof. To see them, we should have had to have flown low over the mat in our Cessna plane.

The tropical forest is not agreeable to walk in. Its interior is as airless and as humid as a hot-house, and it is as dark as the interior of a Gothic cathedral or a Hindu temple on a sunless day. The creepers which hang down, rigidly perpendicular, from hundreds of feet up, give the impression of innumerable slender column-shafts. The forest is gloomy as well as stifling, yet it drew me like a magnet. I made my toilsome way up into it for the first time and got back. I ventured into it a second time and got lost.

This second time, I had crossed a clearing and had plunged back into the forest on the far side of this without having thought of marking my point of entry, and, on reaching the clearing again on what I was intending to be my return journey, I found myself quite unable to identify the direction from which I had originally come. The clearing cannot have been more than a few hundred yards from the forest's edge, where my wife was waiting for me; so I gave a shout; but, even as I shouted, I realized, with dismay, that the forest was drowning my voice, and that I should fail to evoke the answering call that would have reoriented me. All that I could do was to plunge back into the forest at a venture. I started by following the dry bed of a watercourse downwards. This must eventually carry the water, when there was some water in it, out of the forest down to the sea. I soon learnt to avoid this torrent-bed when, in the fading light, I came, in it, to a twenty-foot drop.

We had taken our walk in the cool of the evening; it was now past six o'clock; and Palenque is near enough to the equator for the twilight there to be short. I found that, in spite of myself, I was frightened. I felt as if I had been caught by some malevolent monster that was playing cat and mouse with me. I stumbled on at random, taking a descending course wherever I could, till, at last, to my relief, I came out into a *milpa*—one of those temporary fields, cut out of the bush, from which the Maya snatch a crop. I knew that this field must be accessible from a road, and there was only one road that this could be—the road that wound up to the site of Palenque from the landing-strip. I struck the road a long, long way below the archaeologists' bungalow, and dragged myself home, a sadder and a wiser man.

Our Lady of Guadalupe

IF you have time to see one thing only in Mexico, visit the shrine of Our Lady of Guadalupe on the outskirts of fast-expanding Mexico City. Sacrifice all other objectives for the sake of this one; for here you have the key to Mexico's history since the Spanish conquest. This was a conquest of one cruel race by another. It was more savage even than the subsequent Spanish conquest of Peru. Yet in Mexico the sequel has been a peaceful fusion between the conquerors and the conquered that makes Mexico stand out as a model for all other multiracial countries in the Western World. Mexico has been singularly successful in solving these multiracial countries' common problem; and the cult of Our Lady of Guadalupe has been the most potent of the causes of this Mexican achievement. Over the outer gate into her precincts, you will see inscribed, in the Vulgate text, verse 20 of the hundred-and-forty-seventh psalm: 'He hath not dealt so with any nation.' This proud claim is justified by the historical facts. Our Lady of Guadalupe has been the veritable maker of the unified Mexican nation of today. It is she who has fused two old races together into a new one. She has fused them by creating a union of hearts that has made a mixing of blood acceptable to both parties. The normal present-day Mexican is a mestizo; both pure-blooded Indians and pure-blooded Whites are relatively rare in Mexico. This is Our Lady of Guadalupe's doing. She is deservedly the Mexican people's patron saint—it might be nearer the truth to say 'patron goddess'.

If you are visiting the shrine at Guadalupe from the centre of Mexico City, make sure that you approach the shrine along the pilgrims' way. You will find this thronged; many of the wayfarers on it will have come from afar off; some of them will have come all the way on foot, and will now be doing this last stage of their journey on their knees. Every Latin American, from Chihuahua on the border of the United States to Patagonia, who has any Indian blood in his veins has good reason to honour Our Lady of Guadalupe; for she is the benefactress of the pre-Columbian population of the Americas, not only in Mexico, but throughout the far-flung Latin American World.

When you have passed out of the pilgrims' way through the portal crowned by the proud inscription, you will certainly be dazed and you may even be scandalized, for here you will find, reproduced, to the life, in our present-day world, the scene that once cut Jesus to the heart when he saw it in the Temple at Jerusalem. The same throng of buyers and sellers surrounds you here; and, though the sellers are amiable, they are, no doubt, sharpers, as their Palestinian prototypes were. The pilgrims are poor, but they are numerous, grateful, and open-handed. It is inevitable that human sharks should intercept what they can of the stream of offerings that is flowing towards the gracious goddess's coffers. Do not let yourself be put off; press on from the outer court into the sanctum. Here your heart will be touched by the hundreds of votive paintings that cover the walls. In clumsy strokes and crude colours, these paintings—made by the votaries themselves—depict Our Lady of Guadalupe's miraculous intervention to heal a beneficiary of hers from some sickness or to save him or her from some impending accident. The sincerity of these childlike expressions of gratitude is unmistakable. Here you stand on the threshold of the Holy of Holies.

But how has Our Lady of Guadalupe acquired this mighty power? Who and what is she? She is the Christian Mother of God and at the same time she is Indian—Indian not only in her dress but in the colour of her skin. According to her legend, Our Lady appeared in this guise to an Indian convert to Christianity in the first generation after the conquest. She appeared to him, several times in succession, when he was walking over the ground on which her shrine now stands, and she authenticated the genuineness of these appearances of hers by working a miracle for the convert—a miracle in visible and tangible form which he was able to display to the local Spanish ecclesiastical authorities. After some hesitation, these accepted the miracle as genuine; after some further hesitation, Rome too accepted it. Therewith the legend was now officially established; the shrine at Guadalupe could start on its triumphant career; and the spiritual basis for a reconciliation between the two races had been laid. The goddess of the conquering race had declared herself to be the goddess of the conquered race as well. The story of her beneficent intervention spread far and wide. In any village church in Mexico, you are likely to find a series of pictures portraying the goddess's appearances to the convert and the miracle that she performed, and, in all these pictures, she is given a dusky Indian skin under her Indian clothes.

The spirit for which the shrine of Guadalupe stands was displayed—and, in this case too, in the first generation after the conquest—by Vasco de Quiroga, a noble-minded Spaniard who came to Mexico as a lawyer in the service of the Crown and ended as Bishop of Michoacán. Before leaving Europe, Quiroga had read and taken to heart a recently published book, St. Thomas More's *Utopia*, and he made it his mission to translate More's dream into reality in the newly discovered New World. He found his opening in Western Mexico in the country of the Tarascans—a valiant Indian people who had held their own successfully against the Aztecs but had been crushed, in their turn, by the Spaniards when these had overthrown the Aztec Empire with an impetus that had carried them on beyond its former frontiers. Don Vasco gathered together a fraction of the broken Tarascan people in a settlement of the kind that eventually came to be known as a *reducción* when such settlements were organized for the Indians systematically by the religious orders. He set himself to retrieve his Indian protégés' economic fortunes by teaching them some of the arts and crafts of the Old World that the invaders had brought with them across the Atlantic.

The pattern set by Bishop Vasco de Quiroga's work established a tradition of practical beneficence which was taken up and kept alive by the religious orders and which has survived the violent laicization of Mexican life in the revolution that started in 1910. Today, the tradition is represented by the Casa de Cultura Indigena, whose founding father was the eminent anthropologist Alfonso Caso. I have seen something of this beneficent institution's work among a still primitive Indian people, the Chamulas, whose home is on the Las Casas plateau in the state of Chiapas, in the extreme south-eastern corner of Mexico, next door to Northern Guatemala. The Chamulas' country lies close to the principal seats of the pre-Columbian civilization of Middle America, but the secluded plateau remained beyond this civilization's verge, and the Middle American civilization's successor, the modern Western civilization in Spanish dress, has also not made much impression on the Chamulas yet. At their still rudimentary stage of cultural development, the Chamulas are exposed to the danger of being exploited economically by the Ladinos in their midst. The Casa de Cultura Indigena has undertaken to help the Chamulas, and also other still backward peoples on the other outer edges of Mexico, to find their way into the modern world.

On the Las Casas plateau I visited the local Ladino city, San Cristóbal. I also visited the centre that the Casa de Cultura Indigena has established on the plateau in order to do there, for the Chamulas, what Bishop Vasco de Quiroga did for the Tarascans, four centuries ago. I then went to see the Chamulas on their own ground, but I will keep, for another chapter, what I have to say about this.

San Cristóbal and the other cities of its kind in Spanish America are lineal descendants of the cities planted by Alexander and his Seleucid successors in Asia and by the Romans in Europe. Like their Greek and Roman prototypes, these Spanish cities in the Americas are laid out in a regular grid, with handsome public buildings erected in command-ing positions. Like their prototypes, again, they are alien enclaves in the native social setting into which they have been inserted. At Antioch and at Gadara, the bounds of the exotic Greek language and culture were the walls of the city itself. Aramaic continued to be the language of the country-side, right up to the city-gates. It is the same at San Cristóbal today. The bounds of the Spanish language are here the limits of the urban grid. The whole of the surrounding rural area is Chamula country. The Casa de Cultura Indigena, whose aim is to protect the Chamulas against exploitation by the Ladinos, is actually doing more for the propagation of the Spanish language than the Ladinos of San Cristóbal have ever done. The Casa is training Chamulas to serve as teachers for elementary schools; the instruction given will be very simple; but the language of instruction will be Spanish, not the Chamulas' native language. In Mexico, all education, even the most rudimentary, has, of necessity, to be in Spanish. This is the national language, and the mastery of it is an indispensable qualification for becoming an effective

Mexican citizen. The Spanish language stands for national unity; the Indian languages are legion; some of them are spoken by only an insignificant number of people; and none of them have vocabularies that can convey the ideas and describe the apparatus of modern civilization.

The Casa is also following Bishop Quiroga's lead in training the Chamulas and the Casa's other Indian protégés in the practice of arts and crafts, and it is arranging for them to market their products without the intervention of Ladino middlemen who would have pocketed the profits.

In present-day Mexico, private initiative, as represented by the Casa de Cultura Indigena, does not stand alone in working for the welfare of the primitive elements in the population. I came across a case in which the Government, too, was treating a backward community with comparable benevolence, and was matching its benevolence with an imaginativeness, a patience, and a considerateness that are not a government's characteristic virtues. At Papalo-Apan, in the lowlands adjoining Mexico's Atlantic coast, the Government was building, in 1953, a dam which was to turn the upper part of a river-valley into a reservoir for irrigating the lower part. This project made economic sense, since the soil was barren above the site of the dam, while, below, it was fertile and needed only water to make it productive. The objective was to raise the standard of living of the local Indian population, which was backward and poor. The irrigation of the lower valley from the projected reservoir behind the dam would make it possible for the Indians to cultivate the good soil, which, being, so far, un-irrigated, was neither cultivated nor inhabited yet. There was, however, a human difficulty in the way. The intended beneficiaries of the plan had been living, since time im-memorial, on the bad lands above the site of the dam that were to be submerged under the reservoir; and these poor

Indians were conservative-minded. They were incapable of thinking in terms of improving their economic lot; they were just reluctant to move from their unproductive ancestral home. The Government had, of course, the power to move them compulsorily, but it was not thinking of doing that. Instead, it was sending in a team of anthropologists, who were in the confidence of these Indians and understood the way their minds worked. The Government was proposing to delay the flooding of the upper valley if delay should prove to be needed in order to give time for the anthropologists to persuade the Indians to move of their own accord.

By the date of our visit to Papalo-Apan, some of the Indians had already moved voluntarily to the new houses in the lower valley that had been standing ready to receive them. 'These houses', the authorities explained to me, 'are considerably better than those that they have left, but we have taken care not to make them so much better that the Indians would have been bewildered by the change. When they have got used to living in these houses—say, in about ten years from now—we will build them still better ones; but we shall never force the pace. Our policy is to lead our Indians on gradually towards the goal—and the goal is, of course, assimilation. We want to help them to adapt themselves, with the minimum of strain and pain, to our Mexican national way of life.'

When we went to watch the work on the dam, our eye was caught first by the massive battery of up-to-date machines that were digging and carting and piling at high speed; and then we noticed a number of little men, equipped with nothing better than wheelbarrows and spades, who were dodging between the high-powered mechanical monsters. The contrast prompted me to ask an unintelligent question. 'Why,' I asked, 'when you have all this up-to-date apparatus on the job, do you also employ these manikins? They are merely getting in the way; they are not making any appreciable contribution to the progress of the work. Why hire them and pay them for being a nuisance?' The answer to my unimaginative question put me out of countenance. 'You do not need to tell us', the authorities replied, 'that the employment of this unskilled labour is uneconomic. Our object, in employing it, is not economic; it is psychological. These hands have been recruited from the villages upstream that we want to persuade the Indians to evacuate. One step towards achieving this is to make them feel that the building of the dam is their affair; and they could not be expected to feel this if they had not been allowed to take a share, however minute, in the work. So that is why you see them now working here—and working in their own low-powered traditional way.'

Here we have the bright side of the post-Columbian chapter of Mexican history to set against the dark side. This dark side is dark indeed, but, in partial compensation, the bright side has its highlights; and these present themselves to my mind's eye in two vivid visual memories.

I remember my vision of the landscape, by the shore of Lake Pátzcuaro, in which Bishop Quiroga set himself to translate *Utopia* into real life. I see, once again, the fishermen ceaselessly knitting new nets with an unconscious play of their deft fingers. I see the dense flocks of water-fowl that almost conceal the lake's surface. The birds hardly bother to move out of the way of the boat in which we are heading for the fishing-village on the island. Beyond the lake I see the cone of the volcano Tzintzuntzan. It is a live volcano with wisps of smoke curling upward from its crater. The mountain's graceful curves fill the north-western horizon. And now I am once again breaking my journey from Mexico City to the pyramids of the Sun and Moon at Teotihuacán.

I am turning aside from the road to visit the lovely monastery of Acolman. This was founded, in the next generation after Bishop Quiroga's, by Augustinian fathers. The exquisite carving that adorns the façade of the church was designed by them in the West-European style of their age; but the fathers did not execute their design with their own hands; the work was carried out by Indian apprentices whom the Spanish fathers had trained; and the fineness of the result is evidence that the work was a labour of love.

How were those Indian masons moved to throw themselves into an artistic enterprise that was so alien to their native tradition? I found an answer to my question when I looked out of a window at the peaceful countryside. As I looked, there passed across my field of vision a little troop of animals—a donkey, two cows, and a bunch of sheep and goats—that were being tended, ever so lovingly, by an Indian boy. He, too, was throwing himself into his work, and, for an Indian, this work too, like the sixteenth-century Indian masons' work, was exotic. Like the Plateresque style of the carving on the portal of the church, the entire tribe of the Indian boy's beloved animals was an import from the Old World. Not one of these species had figured among those that had been domesticated by the Indians themselves before the arrival of their European conquerors. Yet it was evident that this twentieth-century Indian boy loved his exotic animals as whole-heartedly as those sixteenth-century Indian masons had loved the exotic style of the work that the Spanish fathers had taught them to do.

No, the conquest was not an unmixed evil. In the evil there was a leaven of something innocently good.

The Gods come back to Life

THE Spanish-speaking peoples of the Americas are all engaged, nowadays, on an identical quest. Every one of them is casting about to find for itself a national essence that will be uniquely its own. The Spanish word for this eagerly sought talisman is *ser*; but the Spanish language and culture will not serve the Spanish-speaking peoples as marks of differentiation. *Hispanidád* is a common property that is shared by all Spain's American offspring with Spain herself. No Spanish-speaking people has a distinctive individuality at this level. The Argentinians are trying to create one for themselves through an apotheosis of the military leaders of their revolt against the Spanish Crown. The Mexicans have a more promising expedient at their command. They are one of the few Spanish-speaking American peoples that can probe down, beneath a Spanish veneer, to a pre-Columbian culture that is peculiar to their own country.

It is true that, in Mexico, the Spanish top-dressing on the national culture is so substantial a crust that it can hold its own against the local pre-Columbian core. The pre-Columbian mound at Cholula may be the biggest artificial mountain in the World; but its pre-Spanish builders' Spanish successors have responded to their predecessors' challenge by building no fewer than three hundred and sixty-five churches at the artificial mountain's foot. The charm of the Spanish city Oaxáca (Waháka) is matched by the beauty of the pre-Columbian works of art that are being disinterred from the innumerable tombs on the natural mountain—Monte Alban—by which Oaxáca is over-shadowed. If Teotihuacán has its massive pyramids of the Sun and Moon, Puebla—Spanish from top to bottom—has the flowery Churrigueresco ornamentation of its ecclesiastical architecture. In fact, Mexico's colonial-age art and architecture can compare with the contemporary performance in Spain and Italy.

However, for a Mexican in search of his national identity, the monuments of this phase of his country's history, imposing though they may be, have one incurable defect. They are not the only monuments of their kind in the New World. Ecuador, Peru, and Brazil can display notable counterparts of them. Accordingly, sophisticated Mexicans have made up their minds that their country's national essence is to be found in the pre-Columbian culture of Middle America, which Mexico shares with no neighbour of hers except Guatemala. This latter-day Mexican cult of Mexico's pre-Columbian past has been fostered by two contemporary events, one in the field of politics and the other in the field of art. Mexico's 'permanent revolution', which started in 1910, has been a radical revolt against the *ancien régime*, and, in the Spanish American World, the *ancien régime* goes back to the Spanish Conquest. This political consideration would have been enough to create a prejudice against the conquerors and all their works in the minds of their alienated descendants; and, as it happens, this revulsion against the Spanish layer of Mexican culture has been given an arresting visual expression in the mighty works of the three great revolutionary-minded Mexican mural-painters: Orozco, Rivera, Siqueiros. These powerful artists have done more than any politicians have to denigrate the post-Cortesian Age of Mexican history and to cloak the pre-Cortesian Age in an aura that gives it the semblance of a golden age when viewed in retrospect through these magicians' transmuting spectacles.

The paradox about this recent cult, in Mexico, of the country's pre-Cortesian past is that its votaries are to be found among the small minority of Mexicans that have an appreciable amount of European blood in their veins. This minority's heroes are the pure-blooded Indians of the age before the conquest; but the descendants of these self-same Indians in the villages on the Mexican plateau are quite unconscious of the esteem in which their ancestral culture has come to be held by a handful of intellectuals in Mexico City. Indeed, they are unaware that there ever was such a thing as a pre-Christian civilization in their country. They have actually been Christians for more than four centuries by now, and they have no recollection of their ever having been anything else. Make a round of the villages in the neighbourhood of Puebla, for instance. You will find that the peasants' life centres on the village church. This will be a sixteenth-century or seventeenth-century building—erected, perhaps, by one of the religious orders. You will find the villagers busying themselves with the upkeep of this heirloom, which is their most highly cherished communal possession. In one village they will be carefully repairing the church's roof; in the next village they will be giving a lick of paint to the head of a stucco cherub in the interior.

These deep-dyed Christian villagers are not going to follow the lead of their sophisticated fellow-citizens who are casting back into the pre-Cortesian past. If their Christian dye does wear thin, they will replace it by another dye of Western origin—the secularism that, since the seventeenth century, has been progressively usurping the traditional place of Christianity in the Western World. On May Day, 1953, on the road between Oaxáca and Mitla, we broke our journey to visit a village church that was deservedly famous for its beauty. That morning the plaza in front of the church was thronged with men and boys, listening to a band playing profane music. For the male population of the village, May Day was now Labour Day, and they were celebrating this. For the women and children, however, May Day was still a saint's day; and, when we entered the church, we found them inside, devoutly paying their respects at the saints' shrines. Since the church was truly beautiful, the women and children had chosen the better part from the aesthetic point of view and (who knows?) perhaps from the spiritual point of view as well.

Thus the Christian peasantry of Central Mexico seems to be showing no inclination to revert to pre-Cortesian paganism. Does this mean that the cult of this pagan past by the Mexican intellectuals can be discounted as a sentimental pose that will have had its day without having made any lasting effect on Mexican life? We might give our question this reassuring answer if the intellectuals and the peasantry, between them, accounted for the whole of the population of Mexico. We have, however, also to reckon with the still primitive elements in the back parts of the country. Till lately, these have been outsiders who have exercised no influence on Mexico's national life. But today, thanks to the benevolent action of the Government, seconded by such private institutions as the Casa de Cultura Indigena, these primitives are being inducted into the national way of life. They are now being 'acculturated'. But is this likely to be just a one-way process? Is it not more probable that, as and when the primitives learn to swim effectively in the national current, they will infect this with a tincture of their own primitive culture which may change the current's colour? In these ex-primitive Mexicans' hearts, may not the pre-Columbian pose of the intellectuals awaken a response that might transform the pose from an ineffectual piece of play-acting into a genuine, and formidable, pagan religious revival?

An outstanding visual presentation of the neo-pre-Columbian pose is the new University City (new when we visited it in 1953; since then, it has become one of the established institutions of the country). The genius of the titanic generation of Mexican artists has decorated this imposing set of public buildings with reproductions of pre-Cortesian Middle American works of art. These reproductions are not just mechanical imitations of the originals. They have not only made faithful copies of the dead art's forms; they have also recaptured and revived its spirit. In this University City, which is frequented, year after year, by thousands of students who are still in their impressionable adolescence, the pre-Christian pantheon of Middle America has been brought back to life. These Middle American gods, like the Etruscan gods, are both terrible and magnetic. Their countenances make you shudder, but their potency grips you before you have time to recoil. This uncanny power of theirs has been brilliantly conjured up again in the decorations of the University City. Is it going to captivate the children or grandchildren of Mexico's ex-primitive citizens, when these eventually find their way to the University?

One of these ex-primitive citizens who was certainly not in danger of being captivated by neo-paganism was the Rector of the University who was in office in 1953. He had been elected to the rectorship on his conspicuous merits. He was an eminent physicist and a first-rate administrator. His academic colleagues of all shades of colour were happy to serve under him, though the Rector himself was an Indian of as dark a hue as Our Lady of Guadalupe.

The Rector's father had made the leap out of Indian poverty into modern middle-class life. The father had been a member of a long family; his own father had died early; and

K

the boy had been left to fend for himself. He had started as a muleteer and had then taken service with a local land-owner. His master was musical; he taught the boy to play; and thereby brought his latent talent to light. One day he was playing in a concert in the state capital, and the governor was in the audience. The governor was so much struck by the boy's performance that he gave him a bursary for the conservatoire in Mexico City. History then repeated itself. The young man's performance at a concert in the national capital, at which the President of the Republic was present, moved the President, in his turn, to give him a bursary, this time for continuing his studies in France. His experience in Paris was discouraging, but the Mexican Ambassador in Paris had the wit to transfer his ward to Germany, where he found a congenial setting for the completion of his musical education. The one-time poor Indian eventually became one of the World's distinguished executants of classical music. I met him in his old age on a trans-atlantic liner, starting out on what may have been his last professional tour. This was the worthy father of a worthy son. This Indian family's spiritual home was the modern world, not pre-Cortesian Middle America.

The Rector and his father were, however, exceptional figures among the Indians from Mexico's backward fringes. They had come from the north; but now travel south-east with me. Take the road from Tuxtla Gutierrez; cross the Grijalva River; climb the steep ascent on to the Las Casas plateau; and, by-passing the Ladino city of San Cristóbal, make for the village of Chamula, which is the civic centre of the Chamula tribe. In this Chamula country, beyond the urban bounds of San Cristóbal, you might fancy yourself to be, not in Latin America, but in some highland canton of South-East Asia. The Chamulas' dress has an Asian look, and so has their gait. They do not walk; they trot, and this with a quaint shamble. As for Chamula village, it must have been laid out originally by a Ladino surveyor; for, unlike the minor villages, some of which I also visited, Chamula village conforms to the regular Latin pattern. It centres on a plaza, with an eighteenth-century church on one side and, flanking it on the two adjoining sides and facing each other, a co-operative store and a clinic, both, of course, recently built.

When you enter the church, you realize that in Chamula-land there is no question of reviving the local pre-Christian religion. This has never died, and by now it has captured the church and the church's contents. The images of the saints have turned into images of the gods; the musical instruments whose strains sound weird to a stranger's ears are accompanying a ritual that is not the Christian liturgy; and the officiants are medicine men, though, to save appearances, they are dubbed 'sacristans'. A priest comes, with some trepidation, once a year from San Cristóbal to celebrate Mass here on sufferance. At the co-operative store the briskest trade is done in candles for burning in honour of the gods in the church-turned-temple. The ex-Christian Cross has parted company with Christ to become a rain-god in its own right. The hills round the village are crowned with rain-god crosses that, in May, were wreathed in supplicatory garlands.

The clinic was new in 1953 and was up-to-date in its equipment. A young doctor, with a medical degree from the University of Mexico, was in charge. I asked him what his prospects were of inducing the Chamulas to take advantage of the facilities for modern medical care that the clinic was now offering to them. 'Well, that', he said, 'does not depend on me. It depends on those "sacristans" whom you have just been seeing in the church. So far, they are still in two minds. They may put the clinic under a ban, and, if they do that, the clinic might as well not have been built and I might as well not stay here. They can put the clinic and me out of action if they choose. Alternatively they may send their sons to receive a modern medical education in the medical faculty of the University in Mexico City, where I was educated myself. They will take whichever of these two possible lines seems to them, on consideration, to be the more promising for the achievement of their objective; and their objective, of course, is to keep their hold over the people.'

Now suppose that the Chamula medicine-men do decide to send their sons to the University. What will be the effect? No doubt, the young men will duly receive a modern medical education in the University's laboratories and in the hospital wards and operating theatres. But what will be the effect on them of the decorations of the University City? May not these potent visual symbols of Middle America's pre-Cortesian religion strike an answering chord in their hearts? May not the effect be to send them back home intellectually post-Christian but more than ever pre-Christian emotionally? May they not take in grim earnest the resurrection of Mexico's pre-Columbian gods—a resurrection that the Mexican intellectuals have been playing with as a *jeu d'esprit*?

If there were indeed to be a genuine revival of Mexico's pre-Cortesian religion, this would be a spiritual disaster; for this religion—at any rate, in its latest phase—is as shocking as it is captivating. The priests of Tenochtitlan—with their hair caked in human blood—shocked even 'stout' Cortés and his men, who were not shocked easily and who were, in fact, themselves found shocking by more sensitive and humane contemporaries of theirs, such as Bishop Quiroga. The Spanish conquerors put the priests to death and made human sacrifice a capital offence; and their verdict on

Middle American religion has been confirmed by posterity—including, until now, the new Mexican nation of mixed Indian and European blood that has been called into existence by Our Lady of Guadalupe.

If the Mexican people, in its search for a distinctive national identity, has to choose, in sober earnest, between an Aztec and a Spanish model for its national image, the Spanish model is surely the less noxious of the two. This conclusion was borne in on me when, on the eve of leaving London for Mexico in 1953, I visited, in London, the exhibition of Mexican art that was touring the World in that year. In this splendid exhibition, all chapters in the history of Mexican art were represented, including the Spanish colonial chapter; and, against the sombre foil of pre-Cortesian Mexican art, the Spanish style, which usually strikes non-Spanish Western eyes as being almost inhumanly austere, looked, in this setting, amiable and almost gay. The pre-Cortesian gods! My memory is still haunted by the gruesomeness of the divinity whose figure confronted the visitor to the exhibition at the entrance. The thought that those fearful gods might perhaps really come back to life again makes me shiver.

The Commonwealth of Puerto Rico

In our troubled present-day World, there are not many spots in which an observer can take satisfaction. The Caribbean island of Puerto Rico is one of these happy exceptions.

Here is a tropical island, in the same chain of islands as Cuba, which is going through a revolution of Cuban magnitude; but this Puerto Rican revolution is of the voluntary peaceful kind that has been achieved in the Scandinavian countries, in Britain, and in the United States too, for that matter, if Americans were willing to take credit for this pacific social revolution of theirs. The importance of the Puerto Rican revolution of our time is that it offers to other Latin American countries a practicable alternative to the violent revolutions that are traditional in that part of the World. Western Europe and North America are too different from Latin America in their way of life to serve as useful examples for Latin American statesmanship to follow. Puerto Rico is in Latin America, besides being in the United States; so what Puerto Rico has achieved is within the other Latin American countries' reach.

Puerto Rico is a country with a dense and rapidly increasing population, but without natural resources. Only a fringe of the island, round the coasts, can raise pineapples and sugar-cane and can attract North American tourists. The interior is pimpled with knobbly wooded hills, rising to mountains towards the south side. If you hover over those barren hills in a helicopter, you spy a tiny field and cottage here and there. But, over the greater part of the country, there is no cultivable land still unutilized. That hilly country will not provide food for extra mouths in search of a livelihood. These must either migrate to New York or find employment in new industries on the island.

Puerto Rico was part of the remnant of the Spanish Empire of the Indies that survived until the close of the last century. Spain must have valued this minor possession of hers, or she would not have built the magnificent seventeenth-century fortifications that still adorn the older part of the island's capital city, San Juán. But Spain neglected most things in Puerto Rico except military defence; and here, as in Cuba, there was a demand for independence before the Spanish-American war brought Spanish rule to an abrupt end. However, for Puerto Rico, unlike Cuba, the outcome was, not independence, but a change of foreign rulers. The United States annexed Puerto Rico without asking the Puerto Ricans' leave, and the next chapter in the story might have been an anti-colonial movement of the familiar kind if, at the critical moment, the Puerto Rican story had not been given a different turn by a remarkable group of liberal-minded and open-minded statesmen.

The first of these was Governor Rexford Tugwell, a continental North American from President Franklin D. Roosevelt's entourage. Governor Tugwell set the peaceful transformation of Puerto Rico in motion, and he picked out, and posted in responsible positions, as young men, several of the Puerto Ricans who are carrying the process of transformation further today. He picked out, for example, Governor Muñoz Marín, who was the governor of the island when I visited it in 1962, and Dr. Jaime Benítez, who had been Chancellor of the University for about twenty years, though he was still in the early prime of life.

Governor Muñoz Marín had come from a distinguished Puerto Rican family with a tradition of resistance to colonial rule which dated back to Spanish times. He might have devoted his energies to opposing the United States, as his father had opposed Spain. Instead, he did some original thinking, and he had the courage to act on it. He came to the conclusion that Puerto Rico's first need was, not to attain political independence, but to raise her people's standard of living—not just the material standard, but the spiritual standard which, in a poor country, cannot be raised unless it is given at least a minimum material foundation. An opening for this was offered by Puerto Rico's relation with the continental United States. The island is, indeed, in a favoured position. Within the United States, Puerto Rico is a politically autonomous commonwealth. The Puerto Ricans pay no U.S. Federal taxes, but the Commonwealth receives Federal grants-in-aid for its public works, and there are no barriers to the entry of Puerto Rican products and immigrants into the continental United States.

One of Governor Muñoz Marín's policies was to make it worth while for continental United States manufacturing corporations to set up subsidiary factories in Puerto Rico. They have been tempted by temporary tax-remissions and by cheap labour, and, though Puerto Rican wage-rates are rising, the local conditions are still favourable enough to make it worth while for United States industry to come to Puerto Rico and to stay there. The consequent new industrial employment on the island has relieved the former pressure on the land, and it has provided a socially healthier outlet than emigration to New York.

In New York, of course, the Puerto Rican immigrants do not have a good name, and no wonder. It is a painful and demoralizing experience for a peasant from some remote rural district to be plunged suddenly into the slums of a giant city. The experience of the Puerto Ricans in New York is unhappily a world-wide phenomenon today; and some healthy practical alternative to deracination and urbanization is one of the most urgent needs of the poverty-stricken peasantry that still constitutes two-thirds or three-quarters of the human race. The launching of local industries in Puerto Rico gives a cue not only for other Latin American countries but for Asian and African countries as well.

Of course, Puerto Rico is not yet out of the wood. In San Juán, shanty-towns jostle with up-to-date luxury apartments and office-buildings. The growth of the population is a constant menace to its prosperity. Yet, comparatively speaking, Puerto Rico is a happy and prosperous country with a promising outlook.

Indian America

THE twenty Latin American republics have in common with each other one urgent and formidable current problem. Next to the avoidance of self-extermination, this problem is the first item on the agenda of perhaps three-quarters of the human race today. It is the common problem of the so-called 'underdeveloped' countries, and it is not the economic problem of harnessing modern applied science to increase a country's productivity. It is the problem of social justice, and this comes first, because, if social justice is lacking, an increase of aggregate wealth will merely make an inequitably rich minority richer than ever, while leaving the poor majority absolutely no better off and relatively poorer.

This was the issue in the recent revolution in Ecuador. It was also the issue in the conference of the Organization of American States that was held, in August 1961, in Uruguay, to implement 'the Alliance for Progress' that had been initiated in March by President Kennedy. The open question is not whether there shall or shall not be a revolution aiming at the achievement of social justice. The present-day movement for social justice is an elemental force, and one of world-wide range. This demand is undoubtedly going to assert itself through one kind of revolution or another. Any attempt to establish social justice is bound to be revolutionary, because the distribution of the benefits of civilization has everywhere been so inequitably unequal in the past. But what kind of a revolution is it to be? This is the open question, and it is a crucial one, because a choice between two different kinds of revolution is being offered to the depressed three-quarters of mankind, and these two prescriptions are in competition with each other.

Social justice can be achieved by a revolution in which a privileged minority consents to a redistribution of wealth in more equitable proportions. The practical possibility of a social revolution of this voluntary, and therefore peaceful, kind is demonstrated by the fact that it has already taken place in a number of North European countries, including Britain. The United States, too, has gone fairly far in the same direction, in spite of the rather doctrinaire North American cult of economic individualism. In the United States, as in Britain, direct taxes, for example, are steeply graded and are effectively collected. The alternative kind of revolution is the penalty to which a country is exposed when the local vested interests obstinately and impenitently refuse to yield to anything short of superior force. And the practicability of this kind of revolution too has been demonstrated by examples. This kind of revolution has already taken place in Russia, China, and Cuba. A revolution of the Cuban type awaits any Latin American country whose ruling minority refuses to carry out a revolution of the British type. This refusal would be a *'gran rifiuto'*, and it would be doubly inexcusable now, because any Latin American country that genuinely and sincerely embarks on a revolution for social justice by peaceful agreement has been assured of generous financial aid from the United States.

On this issue—and it is one of life and death—all Latin American countries are in an identical situation, which they share with most Asian and African countries. Most Latin American countries are also in an identical economic situation. They are agricultural countries that have now entered on the first phase of the Industrial Revolution. At the same time, the Latin American countries fall into two groups when we look at the composition of their populations. There is one group in which the present population is, like that of the United States and Canada, mainly derived from the Old World—mostly from Europe but partly from Africa as well. In Latin America, this group of countries includes not only Argentina, Chile, and Uruguay, but also Brazil, Venezuela, Colombia, and Costa Rica. The other group consists of countries in which the present population is mainly native American in race, with a relatively small infusion of European and African blood. This group includes Mexico, Guatemala, most of the other Central American republics except Costa Rica, and, in South America, Ecuador, Peru, Bolivia, and Paraguay. In all these countries there are culturally unassimilated 'Indian' elements in the population, which complicate their social structure and give a special character to the local demand for social justice.

Bolivia is the Latin American country with the largest quota of unassimilated Indians. Here they amount to about 90 per cent of the whole population. Bolivia is also the first Indian-American country in which the unassimilated Indian community has asserted itself in a revolution that has been fairly violent. They have broken up the former large estates and have resumed possession of the land. This has happened since 1952—and it was overdue; for, by then, more than four hundred years had passed since the Indian peasantry of what is now Bolivia was crushed by the Spanish conquest of the Empire of the Incas.

In Latin American countries that contain still unassimilated Indian communities, these remain outside the pale of the national life. Their position was not changed by the war of independence against Spain which brought the Latin American republics into existence in the early years of the nineteenth century. All that then happened, from the

Indians' point of view, was that they became the subjects of the local Spanish-descended *latifundarios* (mammoth landlords) instead of the Spanish Crown. Till our own time the political and social structure of most Latin American republics has remained hierarchical; and even in Mexico, which has been officially in a state of 'permanent revolution' since 1910, agrarian reform is still far from complete. In 1950, 42·2 per cent. of the agricultural workers in Mexico were reported to be still working for others, without having any land-holdings of their own.

In the social and economic hierarchy of the Indian-American countries, the unassimilated Indians are at the bottom of the scale. But, in Indian-America, class-divisions do not coincide with racial differences, as they do in the Old South of the United States and in a number of southern, central, and eastern African countries. An unassimilated Indian can 'pass' (to use the North American word) with an ease that would be the envy of a Negro in the United States or in the Union of South Africa. If he learns to talk Spanish, takes to wearing present-day Western clothes, and migrates from his village to the city, he can become a Ladino—that is to say, an acknowledged member of modern civilized society in the Hispanic version of it. And, in a republic in which social injustice is punctuated—and occasionally punctured—by violent revolution, any Ladino may, with luck, rise high, even if, in race, he is pure Indian, and not of mixed Indian and European blood, as the majority of the population is by now in Mexico and Peru.

What is to be the future of the Indian community in Ecuador, for instance? Standing at the door of the cathedral in Quito, I have watched Indian men and women shambling in and out self-consciously and apologetically, as if they had no right to show their faces in the capital of what is officially their country. On the other hand, in go-ahead Guayaquil, I have seen other Ecuadorian Indians becoming effective modern technicians and earning wages that would still seem fabulous to their brothers who have stayed at home in the ancient Indian villages in the Ecuadorian highlands. The wind of change is blowing hard now through Indian America. Like truth, the demand for social justice is mighty; and, by the violent kind of revolution if not by the peaceful kind, it is assuredly going to prevail.

Towards Integration in Latin America?

IN our time the World is being carried towards unification by the ever-accelerating progress of technology. This seems to be an irresistible force; and, if it is irresistible, it is formidable; for technology is morally neutral. Technology puts increasing power into human hands for human wills to wield, as they may choose, either for good or for evil. We may use a World that technology has unified for us as an arena for committing mass-suicide by fighting an atomic world-war. Alternatively we may turn a unified World into a common home in which the whole human race can live, for the first time, like a single family. The two alternatives that technology offers to us are poles apart, and the choice between these two extremes will not be made by technology; it will be made by us.

If, in the Atomic Age, the human race's alternative to self-destruction is to become a single family, this requires the establishment of at least the rudiments of a world-government. We are still far from achieving this. The essence of government, on any scale, is power. A government is not a government if it has not the power to compel municipal authorities, as well as individual citizens, to obey its orders. A world-government that is effective in this crucial sense is not yet in the making. What are the World's political prospects? At present we are witnessing a tug-of-war between a process of 'Balkanization' and a process of consolidation in which splinter-states coalesce into larger units whose dimensions may be regional but still fall far short of being world-wide.

The process of 'Balkanization', which has doubled the number of this planet's sovereign independent states since the end of the Second World War, did not begin in the Balkans. It began in the Spanish Empire of the Indies. This broke up into successor-states (the number of these is now eighteen) before the same fate overtook the Spanish Empire's Levantine contemporary and rival the Ottoman Empire. Since then, the Austrian, French, and British Empires have gone the same way.

When a small people that has been incorporated in a large empire wins independence, its first reaction is to rejoice in this new status—especially in cases in which the winning of independence has cost an arduous struggle. In the next stage, the experience of independence may lead to second thoughts; for everything has its price; and, for a small country, the price of independence may be a political and economic impotence that places this nominally sovereign community at the mercy of stronger powers as effectively as if the country were still a subject territory. The obvious antidote to local sovereign impotence is some form of voluntary reunification, and, today, this ideal is hovering before the minds of the people of the Arab successor-states of the Ottoman Empire, the tropical African successor-states of the French and British Empires, and the Latin American successor-states of the Spanish and Portuguese Empires. Undoubtedly a united Arab world, a united tropical African world, and a united Latin American world would each be in a stronger bargaining position, vis-à-vis of the super-powers, than the separate Arab, tropical African, and Latin American states now are individually.

This is unquestionable, but it does raise two questions—one preliminary and the other ulterior. The preliminary question is whether, in any of these three cases, voluntary unification on a regional scale is practical politics; the ulterior question is whether consolidation on a regional scale will help or hinder the unification on a world-wide scale which, in the Atomic Age, is probably mankind's only alternative to self-destruction. The Latin American countries have experienced the drawbacks, as well as the advantages, of separate national independence for a longer time than either the Arab countries or the tropical African countries. By now, most of the Latin American republics have been sovereign independent states for about a century and a half. The present feelings of the Latin American peoples may therefore give us a preview of the future feelings of the Arab and the tropical African peoples.

In Latin America a new desire for unification has declared itself quite recently. This is most manifest in the economic field, but it can be seen in the cultural field as well. For instance, in October 1966 a congress of Latin American historians was held in Buenos Aires under the auspices of the Argentinian Academy of History. Political unification is the moot question. The experience of the present six members of the European Common Market shows that, under modern conditions, economic unification cannot be carried far without a substantial accompanying measure of political unification. Are the Latin American peoples yet prepared, on the political plane, to make any sacrifices of national sovereignty?

By now I have visited eleven Latin American countries: Mexico, Guatemala, Panamá, Colombia, Venezuela, Ecuador, Peru, Brazil, Uruguay, Argentina, Chile. My impression, for what it is worth, is that, since they achieved independence, the Latin American republics have been growing farther and farther apart from each other. This has been an inevitable result of separate sovereign independence, but separateness has also been deliberately cultivated. In some Latin American countries, the nineteenth-century national liberators are now not just venerated as heroes: they are worshipped as veritable gods. Nationalism has, indeed, become a more potent religion than Christianity. When one visits these temples of nationalism, one sees processions of school-children being led up by their teachers to be indoctrinated. If this indoctrination is not counteracted by the inculcation of some less narrow loyalty, these children seem likely to grow up as incorrigible nationalists. They will be resistant to the call for regional integration, not to speak of the call for unity on a world-wide scale. If I were a Latin American integrationist, my first step would be to dump all the statues of San Martín in the Atlantic, all the statues of O'Higgins in the Pacific, and all the statues of Bolívar in the Caribbean, and I would forbid their replacement, under pain of death. I would substitute for them replicas of the Christ of the Andes and pictures of the Virgin of Guadalupe, and I would promote voluntary—not compulsory—pilgrimages of school-children to these.

Now let us suppose that, in Latin America, the wish for integration does prevail over nationalism. Is this going to open the way towards a wish for world-unity, or is it going merely to replace splinter-nationalism by a more vicious regional super-nationalism? This is still an open question. but the sequel to the nineteenth-century unification of Germany is a bad augury.

Index

152 *Between Maule and Amazon*

*Printed in Great Britain
by The Camelot Press Ltd.,
London and Southampton*